CW01481141

*Israel:*

# THE LAND IN CONTROVERSY

*A biblical approach*

## Claude Ezagouri

Copyright © 2013 by Claude Ezagouri

*Israel: THE LAND IN CONTROVERSY*
*A biblical approach*
by Claude Ezagouri

Printed in the United States of America

ISBN 9781628712452

All rights reserved solely by the author. The author guarantees all contents are original and do not infringe upon the legal rights of any other person or work. No part of this book may be reproduced in any form without the permission of the author. The views expressed in this book are not necessarily those of the publisher.

Unless noted otherwise, scripture quotations are from the Holy Bible, New International Version ®. Copyright © 1973, 1978, 1984 by International Bible Society. Used by permission of Zondervan Publishing House.

Scriptures marked NKJV are from the New King James Version. Copyright © 1982 by Thomas Nelson, Inc. Used by permission. All rights reserved.

www.xulonpress.com

# ACKNOWLEDGEMENTS

I thank God for His anointing and guidance as I wrote the book. My appreciation also goes to Barbara Mayer for editorial advice and her husband Gary for his exemplary friendship. And finally, my thanks goes to my wife Michelle and my daughter Guitit for their assistance.

# TABLE OF CONTENTS

# Introduction

This book has been written at a time when Israel is being scrutinized and criticized by all the world media. It is no secret that in history the Jewish people have continually been the focus of attack, whether physically, culturally or spiritually. There always seemed to be a reason why the Jews deserved torture, deportation, destitution or even annihilation. During the Second World War Hitler was convinced that the Jews went too far in their control of Europe and there had to be a final solution. What ensued after that was one of the most horrific acts of hatred and cruelty in the history of the human race. After the war, almost everyone in the whole world was convinced that the Jewish people had been at least unfairly treated. Therefore the nations thought it wise to give them, who had wandered from country to country for close to 2000 years, a land where they would live in peace and govern their own affairs. However as soon as the Jews regained claim of the land of their forefathers in 1948, they encountered the fierce opposition of their surrounding enemies. At that time the borders of Israel were hardly the ones that had been agreed upon by the United Nations, which tells us that the enemies' belligerence was not based on a territorial dispute but rather on their utter refusal of the Jews' possession of even an inch of land in the Middle East.

Today as Islam takes an extreme form of fundamentalism, there have been successful attempts to convince people and even nations that the Jews have no legitimacy on their land any longer. Yet, at the time when the nations are proposing their plan for a just solution to the Middle East puzzle, God is inexorably unfolding *His* plan already announced from Genesis. This discrepancy between the nations' schemes and God's will is at the centre of people's wrong evaluation of the events unfolding in this region of the world and will probably precipitate the nations into a direct confrontation with the Lord of the whole earth. It is therefore urgent for the world to identify the enemy's plan to deceive the nations and for the Church to discern God's will and the actual relevancy of the scriptures in this respect. The leaders' mistakes, the passion and the emotions of this conflict, the zeal of both sides and the drama of the hour on the ground tend to pull us away from God's word and His promises not only for Israel but also for the rest of the world. As we follow the development of events in the Middle East in the light of the Bible, we need to discern the nature of the conflict and its trend. First, it is expedient to grasp the historical, emotional and spiritual umbilical cord that exists between the Jewish people and the land. Then it is useful to identify the validity of the biblical prophecies today as well as the important issue of the borders according to God's plan. We will also look into the complicated reality as we come to grips with a peace process for the Middle East. This is why this book seeks to bring God's word in abundance for justification of every thought, rather than to vent opinions that would only confuse the mind. It will also be good to state the facts on the ground in order to avoid a biased attitude based on politically correct reports.

The relationship between the Church and Israel, together with the growing Messianic movement of Jewish believers in Israel will have to be reevaluated. This equation actually presents an excellent hope for the whole world if only the Church would endeavour to understand the Lord's heart and plan through the end time biblical prophecies. We are living in crucial times for the whole world but a lot will depend on the nations' stance on the existence and the borders of the land of Israel. It is therefore indispensable to study God's word regarding this matter and this is one of the main purposes of this book.

*Chapter 1*

# UNDERSTANDING THE CONCEPT OF THE LAND

## The land under God's scrutiny

I n His infinite love and His immense wisdom, God created the heavens and the earth but the earth lies as His cherished jewel before Him. Are not the heavens His throne and the earth His footstool? Isn't He invariably heedful to any event that occurs on the surface of the globe? Yet He often stresses His particular attention on a tiny territory there in the Middle East:

> *It is a land the LORD your God cares for; the eyes of the LORD your God are continually on it from the beginning of the year to its end (Deuteronomy 11:12).*

In Hebrew the word translated *continually* is *tamid* which simply means *always*. This implies that God's care for the land is not just historical but rather immutable, as long as there is life upon this land. Today as in Bible times, the land of Israel is more than ever present in the Middle East and its people still dwell there, surrounded by enemies as it was in Old Testament times. Here again the word *land* applies to the territory which was promised to the patriarchs and where God brought the 12 tribes of Israel. This verse is specifically about the land of Canaan; it is *the land you are entering to take over* (Deuteronomy 11:10). Therefore, although it is true that nothing escapes God's attention on the surface of the earth, the point that is made here is about how close God is to this specific piece of land and how everything that pertains to this land is so precious to His eyes and heart. This is something to bear in mind nowadays as the nations seem to assume that God is now turning His attention to the whole world and is therefore not anymore particularly interested in the land of Israel. In many Christian circles, there is the belief that Messiah's first coming caused the Lord to become drastically oblivious of His past love for Israel and for His land. With this kind of reasoning, it is easy to conclude that every truth, every concept in the scriptures is now universalized and spiritualized, therefore any relation between God and the people of Israel has become futile and irrelevant. This has very serious negative implications for our faith because, by showing unfaithfulness to His people in a way not aligned with the scriptures, He would jeopardize His faithfulness to His Church and to every one of us.

The fact that God focuses on such a tiny piece of land when He owns the whole earth is in itself interesting, to say the least. From the beginning to the end of the Bible, we see God stoop down to the micro although He is definitely the master of the macro. While He rules the earth, the stars, the seasons and all the galaxies in the immensity of the universe, He still chooses a tiny land and a small people to work out His will through them. This is His way to show that He is an accessible king, a Lord who keeps close to His minute creation. He is interested in the puny life of small creatures like ants and indeed like men. Nothing escapes His attention on the face of the globe. This concept climaxed when He came to His land to live in the midst of His people. What we generally tend to forget, reading Yeshua's life (Jesus' life) and ministry on earth, is His choice of land to manifest His glory. If, as some tend to believe, there was a drastic disconnect between the Old and the New Covenant, Yeshua could have been born in Uganda and demonstrated His ministry first to the Gentiles. However although Uganda was already in His heart at that time, it is significant that He came first to the lost sheep of Israel and that His gospel was to the Jews first. His chosen proximity to the land of Israel must have been a wonder to those who discerned His true identity as the promised Messiah. Even more puzzling is the way He related to the land. He wept as He came to Jerusalem, He sweated blood in Gethsemane, He ruled over the Sea of Galilee, dictating His will to the waves. He used His long walks through the land of Israel to teach, rebuke, guide, heal and deliver. He was so observant of the birds and the flowers that He used them as examples in His parables. It is undeniable that Yeshua was aware of the extreme beauty of nature in this piece of land as something which would unfailingly catch the wanderer's attention. He knew the history of the land and of its people and He commented on it:

> *Now there were some present at that time who told Jesus about the Galileans whose blood Pilate had mixed with their sacrifices. Jesus answered, "Do you think that these Galileans were worse sinners than all the other Galileans because they suffered this way? I tell you, no! But unless you repent, you too will all perish. Or those eighteen who died when the tower in Siloam fell on*

*them — do you think they were more guilty than all the others living in Jerusalem? I tell you, no! But unless you repent, you too will all perish." Luke 13:1-5*

His closeness to and knowledge of this particular piece of land was a tool in His hands to administer precious teaching in love to His listeners. Although His first abode was His Father's kingdom, Yeshua definitely felt at home on His land and His spirit is still at home in a land where His people are back today. In the same way as He wept over Jerusalem, He is weeping today at the sight of the wars, terrorist attacks and the suffering of both Arabs and Jews. His eyes are on every event, every stone and on every Jew, because it is this people He chose among all nations to fulfill His will:

*"For you are a people holy to the LORD your God. The LORD your God has chosen you out of all the peoples on the face of the earth to be his people, his treasured possession" (Deut. 7:6).*

Israel depends on the Lord for everything and the Israelis know it in their deepest inner being. They certainly depend upon Him for water: every year the Israelis pray for rain, sometimes in such a fervent and desperate way that it is publicly announced on the Israeli TV news. God sees to it that the Sea of Galilee, Israel's main water reservoir, is filled by rains in due time. Even when the level of the lake comes very close to the red alert level, God has always replenished it. In 2011, after a few years of drought, even the experts advised to stop pumping water from the Sea of Galilee because the level was five meters beneath the normal one. Fishing

16

was forbidden for one year and the government was already trying to find other solutions for water supply. In contrast, the winter of 2013 was so exceptionally rainy that the lake was almost replenished, something that very few people would have expected. God was in control and He did not let the ecology of the Sea of Galilee deteriorate. He was heedful to provide the country with enough water supplies from His heavenly reservoirs.

He cannot be heedless when threats of destruction are heard from Iran or from other enemies of Israel. He is always there not only to answer prayer but also to intervene if anything should come to change the course of events in a way that would thwart His promises and His word. The future of this land and of this people is not and cannot be controlled by the UN or any group of nations. God is still sovereign upon His own land and this is why He is so close to it. Every decision taken by the nations concerning this particular land will always be used by God to serve His purposes toward the fulfillment of the end time biblical prophecies and to the glory of His name. In our present age when man thinks he is in control of the whole earth through his technology and science, God lifts up His standard and reminds mankind of His full dominion in a particular way on the land He called His own.`

**It is God's land**

Israel is a special land and this is why many have tried and are still trying to own it. In any country in the world, land can be purchased and inherited for ever. To this day one cannot buy a piece of land in Israel and own it for more than 49 years. At the end of 49 years of ownership, it would have to be redeemed again. This principle finds its source in some Torah commandments:

*"You are to buy from your countryman on the basis of the number of years since the Jubilee. And he is to sell to you on the basis of the number of years left for harvesting crops" (Lev. 25:15.)*

We need to understand that this command is based on another important passage of scriptures:

*"The land must not be sold permanently, because the land is mine and you are but aliens and my tenants" (Lev. 25:23).*

Some commentators have raised the assumption that the word *aretz* in the Old Testament can describe the land of Israel but also the whole earth. Indeed this is a valid remark that ought to be considered as we can see in the following verse:

*"The earth is the LORD's, and everything in it, the world, and all who live in it;" (Ps. 24:1).*

Here it makes little doubt that God refers to His Lordship on the whole earth as the creator and owner of the universe. While this is true, the law about the land in Leviticus 25:23 is part of the Torah which was given to the Israelites after He set them free from the bondage of slavery in Egypt. Therefore it applies specifically to the Jewish people and the land of Israel where God was leading His people to settle:

18

*Therefore, say to the Israelites: "I am the LORD, and I will bring you out from under the yoke of the Egyptians. I will free you from being slaves to them, and I will redeem you with an outstretched arm and with mighty acts of judgment. I will take you as my own people, and I will be your God. Then you will know that I am the LORD your God, **who brought you out from under the yoke of the Egyptians. And I will bring you to the land** I swore with uplifted hand to give to Abraham, to Isaac and to Jacob. I will give it to you as a possession. I am the LORD."*
*Exodus 6:6-8*

As we can see at the beginning of the chapter, Leviticus 25:23 was spoken to the Israelites. It was important for God to let them know that this land belonged to Him, and nobody would contest the legitimacy of this truth today. Although it is part of the torah, it is still valid and is part of God's word. This was a significant assumption because of the possibility that the land could have been sold to get something else in return. We can see an obvious principle here: we cannot sell something that doesn't belong to us, and this is all the more true when its owner is the Lord of all the earth. Although this principle seems very logical as a general standard, it is astounding how misinterpreted and biased it becomes when dealing with the land of Israel, as the nations of the world are so quick to suggest the exchange of pieces of God's land for a so-called peace:

19

> *"They dress the wound of my people as though it were not serious. 'Peace, peace', they say, when there is no peace." (Jer. 6:14).*

In fact, God doesn't only remind Israel about His ownership of the land but He also flares at the nations who violate this important principle:

> *This is what the Sovereign LORD says: In my burning zeal I have spoken against the rest of the nations, and against all Edom, for with glee and with malice in their hearts **they made my land their own possession** so that they might plunder its pastureland. Ezekiel 36:5*

This should be recalled today when governments of the world are discussing different ways to divide and redistribute God's land to nations other than Israel. In its utter ignorance of the Bible, the world is heading to a perilous confrontation with the Master of the universe. At a time when the Bible is translated in most of the languages of the world and accessible by everyone on the planet, ignoring its content is not an excuse before God.

But while the nations continue in their ignorance and are leaving God out of the picture, a significant section of Christianity has developed the apparently legitimate idea that, while this law of Leviticus 25:23 can be applied individually, it cannot apply to Israel as a nation. However the Lord, speaking to the Israelites through His servant Moses, did say that they are considered as tenants on the land, indicating that they didn't have the authority to sell it, but they did have the responsibility to keep it. We see this principle recur several

20

times in different passages of the scriptures, starting with Adam who was supposed to tend the Garden of Eden and enjoy it without taking full ownership of it. In some parables of the gospel we often see that the owner of a certain property goes away but leaves his tenants there to take care of it. Consequently, they are held responsible for any eventual damage when the Landlord returns.

One could misunderstand Leviticus 25:23 by assuming that since the land belongs to the Lord, it does not belong to anyone else, Israel included. While this is not far from the truth, God chose the Israelites, who happen to be the forefathers of the modern Jewish people, to be responsible tenants of the land and take care of it. The matter that will need to be determined is whether this responsibility was given to Israel for a season or forever and we will try to deal with this question further on. Anyway, one thing that seems to come out of the reading of the Bible is the close relationship that God establishes between the land and His people:

*"You showed favour to your land, O LORD;*
*you restored the fortunes of Jacob" (Ps. 85:1).*

God is keen to bless His land, but He often shows the extent of His favour through the restoration of the people of the land.

Similarly, the land is so intertwined with its people that whenever it is profaned by sin, God brings an enemy not only against the people but also against the land:

*"You will advance **against my people Israel** like a cloud that covers the land. In days to come, O Gog, **I will bring you against my land**, so that the nations may know me when*

*I show myself holy through you before their eyes" (Ezek. 38:16).*

In other words, it is virtually impossible to separate the land from God's people, as some are tempted to do. Although the term *Zionism* has become a byword around the world today, it reflects the biblical principle according to which this particular land was not supposed to be desolate but rather inhabited by God's people. This is so true that it becomes a factor of protection, even of survival for the Jews. Indeed. Following 2000 years of persecution against the Jews, even the United Nations decided that enough was enough. Therefore, they allowed the Jews to take refuge in their own land and develop their own army. The attempts to separate the Jewish people from the land of Israel raise some suspicions whether anti-Zionism is not intrinsically an unaware but subtle form of anti-Semitism. We are not suggesting here that anti-Zionism is purposely anti-Semitism, but its stand presupposes that the Jews have no legitimate biblical right to the land of Israel. This indirectly, perhaps unknowingly suggests that they should return to the nations where they came from or live on their land under a foreign leadership. When we recall the 2000 years of persecution that the Jews endured in these nations, we can only tremble at the thought of their return to the past, let alone of being overruled by another people in Israel.

Moreover, it is crucial to understand the responsibility deeply felt within the Jewish heart concerning the land. This sense of responsibility is bolstered by the Jews' profound awareness of the land belonging to God. For centuries, this notion has been part of the Jewish religious mindset and can be traced back to the patriarchs as Lance Lambert wrote:

*Jacob may have had a lot of problems with the strength of his own nature, with his self will, with his zeal to get things done, but there was one thing about Jacob: he had regard for the things of God. Deeper than his twistedness, deeper than his deceit, deeper than his business acumen and shrewdness was this desire for the things of God. That was why he wanted the birthright – he valued it. That was why he stole the blessing – he saw the value of it. That was why he understood God's promise about the land and why, when it seemed famine had come to the whole area and there was plenty of food in Egypt, he was not prepared to go down there. He would prefer to stay in the land in a time of famine, somewhat believing that God would meet them.[1]*

This sense of responsibility to keep and take care of the land until the coming of the Messiah became even more acute after the establishment of the State of Israel through a vote in the United Nations. It is quite astounding that the representatives of the nations in the UN at that time, who had no belief in God's word, could take such a decision. It undoubtedly suggests God's hand upon them to cast such an inspired vote. The Jews are generally astonished that Christians, who are supposed to base their lives on the Bible, would be among the ones who encourage them to relinquish the whole land or even sections of it. Not finding any explanation for this Christian theological attitude, they put it on the account of traditional Christian anti-Semitism. This is a sad fact that remains an obstacle to the salvation of the Jews to this very day. In the Jewish mind, adopting Christianity means embracing an expression of anti-Semitism, and they see their possession of the land as a shield against the dangers of persecutions. Knowing the historical position of the Church in this matter, this is not something that the Jews are ready to take lightly. It also provokes their anger against the Messianic believers who are regarded as traitors taking sides with a sort of Christianity that they consider antagonist to the future and existence of the Jewish people. It is only when Christians show their love to Israel that this sentiment tends to subside.

**The land is holy**

> *"Thus he brought them to the border of **his holy land**, to the hill country his right hand had taken. He drove out nations before them and allotted their lands to them as an inheritance; he settled the tribes of Israel in their homes." (Ps. 78:54-55).*

Israel is not a land like any other land. Its holiness requires a holy people and this is the main reason why God had to first do away with the unholy nations living upon the land to work out His will through a people of His choice. Some of the early Church fathers had a hard time understanding and receiving this principle. For instance Marcion saw in the pages of the Old Testament a cruel God of battles and bloody sacrifices and to this day, these passages of scriptures are stumbling blocks for many believers who cannot comprehend how a God of love and peace could send His people to make war and destroy other nations. Steve Maltz wrote:

24

*The Israelites were meant to be a holy nation, a nation under God, a theocracy. They were chosen to be a nation apart, living among the other nations, but apart from them. This is why it was for their own good to destroy the corrupt nations around them: not to satisfy the apparent bloodlust of the deity, but to keep God's people as pure and uncorrupted as possible. However, it was never going to be easy.[2]*

God finds it difficult to accept an unholy nation upon His holy land. Of course, here comes the necessity for the people to be holy according to God's criteria. The fact that this principle is humanly impossible does not decrease its importance. It only reveals the need of God's intervention to make the impossible possible. It was thus necessary for the Lord to give the people a framework of laws destined to keep it somehow righteous so that they might be allowed to live on the land. This was an elaborate written code with precepts and commandments that inspired the judges of the whole world later in the course of history. Being aware of the difficulty for His people to abide by His system of laws and attain holiness, God seems to keep a sacred place for Himself within the borders of the holy land:

*"When you allot the land as an inheritance, you are to present to the LORD **a portion of the land as a sacred district**, 25,000 cubits long and 20,000 cubits wide; the entire area will be holy." (Ezek. 45:1).*

Here this is seen in prophecy by the prophet Ezekiel and it already reveals that, as we shall see further on,

God has a plan for His land on which He intended to have the *sanctuary* (verse 2) because He meant to bring His people to His land for worship:

> *"You will bring them in and plant them on the mountain of your inheritance — the place, O LORD, you made for your dwelling, the sanctuary, O Lord, your hands established."*
> *(Ex. 15:17).*

It is easy to believe in a holy kingdom somewhere in the heavens where God reigns eternally. However, people generally find it hard to accept that God can make His dwelling on this depraved earth, even on a piece of ground that He chose for his future reign on the earth. However if this is really what the scriptures tell us, isn't it logical today that God would be able to sanctify the same land of Israel where He was so active both in Old Testament and New Testament times? In fact, if God's plan from the beginning was for His people to be holy, it was His desire to bring the Israelites to a holy place.

Furthermore, we see in the scriptures that God often personalizes the land in an intimate way. It is not automatically sanctified holy by the people's holiness but it is inherently holy, however often profaned by Israel. Therefore the Jews had to be exiled to Babylon, not only because of their sins against God but also because of their sins against the land:

> *"The land enjoyed its sabbath rests; all the time of its desolation it rested, until the seventy years were completed in fulfillment of the word of the LORD spoken by Jeremiah."*
> *(2 Chron. 36:21).*

If the Lord is so watchful for His land, we can assume how difficult it is to separate the sin of Israel from the trials that this people endured. God is very zealous for His people but He is not less zealous for His land. Therefore, being chosen by God to live upon His land implies a way of life and conduct that are acceptable to Him. However, because of the narrow connection between the country and its often corrupted people, it is logical and necessary for the land to be redeemed.

**The land is redeemed**

God's solemn declaration that the land belongs to Him is sealed and confirmed by a significant biblical practice according to which it had to be cleansed and redeemed from sin. In order to understand this practice we need first to consider the fact of the desecration of the land. God knew that His decision to allow men to settle upon His land would cause its profanation, especially by the shedding of blood in murders, wars and sin in general:

> *"I brought you into a fertile land to eat its fruit and rich produce.* ***But you came and defiled my land and made my inheritance detestable."*** *(Jer. 2:7).*

The land is often personalized in such a way that it cries out to the Lord after the shedding of innocent blood. This was the case after Abel was murdered by his brother:

> *"The LORD said, 'What have you done? Listen!* ***Your brother's blood cries out to me from the ground'"*** *(Gen. 4:10).*

27

How can God allow His land to be defiled especially when His ultimate holy purpose is to send His Son back to reign on it? In anticipation of this glorious advent, He often calls His land holy, but in order for it to remain holy despite sin and the shedding of blood, He had to redeem it. The ultimate redemption of the land took place in Jerusalem. This is the city chosen by God for the shedding of His Son's blood and we have several glimpses of this factor of redemption in the scriptures. Yeshua redeemed the land by the shedding of His blood in Gethsemane:

> *"And being in anguish, he prayed more earnestly, and his sweat was like drops of blood **falling to the ground."** (Luke 22:44).*

These drops were shed without the use of the lictors' scourge, the crown of thorns, the nails or the spear of the Roman soldier and this blood fell on the ground with no violence inflicted to the Saviour because it was offered as the first fruit of His love for mankind. It was also important that his blood fell upon the ground for cleansing.

We already see a glimpse of this principle in the book of Genesis. When God reiterated His promise of the land to Jacob, this is what Jacob did:

> *"Jacob set up a stone pillar at the place where God had talked with him, and he **poured out a drink offering on it**; he also poured oil on it. Jacob called the place where God had talked with him **Bethel."** (Gen. 35:14-15).*

This act was some kind of sacrifice but Jacob knew somehow that this piece of land had to be sanctified not only because it was *the house of God,* but also in view of the future inheritance promised by the Lord. Moreover, further on, God is much more specific about this sanctification and redemption of the land which He links to His people:

*"Rejoice, O nations, with his people, for he will avenge the blood of his servants; he will take vengeance on his enemies and* **make atonement for his land and people.***" (Deut. 32:43).*

Notice that God makes this declaration to the nations. He turns to call them to rejoice not only over the redemption of the land but also over the link that He establishes here between His land and the people of Israel. The Lord intends to warn the world against any indignation or jealousy toward Israel because of God's choice. He seems to challenge the nations to understand that His overall and final plan for the land and His people is for the benefit and redemption of the whole world. God confronts the enemies of Israel with the redemption not only of His land but also of the people whom He chose for the fulfillment of His will. Not only the land but also its people must be redeemed in order for God to be able to work out His plan to reign from Jerusalem and bless the nations from Zion. The link of the land to the people has much to do with the redemption of both. This includes the wonderful promise of eternal salvation that He has provided for Israel:

**"But Israel will be saved by the LORD with an everlasting salvation;** *you will never be put to shame or disgraced, to ages everlasting." (Is. 45:17).*

The salvation of erring Israel is crucial in the fulfillment of God's final plan for mankind. The Jewish People are the only one on the face of the earth with a specific promise of everlasting salvation or redemption in God's word. Of course, this does not implicitly mean that the other nations will not be saved, but it was necessary for God to stress this particularity as we will discuss in the following chapters.

As a matter of fact, the linkage made by our Lord between the land and the people is often underestimated or misunderstood. It is undeniable that the land needed either to remain holy or to be redeemed before the Lord. When Ezra and Nehemiah received the God-inspired burden to rebuild Jerusalem, their first task was the edification of the temple. The returned captives could not even consider a resettlement on the land without a holy place and this specific location was pivotal to the rest of the work. It was toward this place that the prayers went and till today the Jews pray with their face turned toward the holy city as in David's time.

*"I will bow down **toward your holy temple** and will praise your name for your love and your faithfulness, for you have exalted above all things your name and your word."* (Ps. 138:2).

This temple inspired the scribes and the psalmists and the loss of this sacred place caused the people to lament bitterly:

*"For a little while your people possessed your holy place, but now our enemies have trampled down your sanctuary." (Is.63:18).*

Noah, Abraham, Isaac, Jacob, Moses and Gideon were not the only ones to build an altar in strategic places in relation with the occupation of the land and they knew that every inch of ground had to be won by sacrifice. Often the slaughter of an animal and the shedding of its blood on the altar stopped God's wrath at the very same place. This is precisely what David did to stop the plague:

> *"Araunah said, 'Why has my lord the king come to his servant?' 'To buy your threshing floor,' David answered, 'so I can build an altar to the LORD, that the plague on the people may be stopped.'" (2 Sam. 24:21).*

The redemption of the land was a prerequisite for the people to settle on it and for this holy union between the land and the people to be wrought.

## Chapter 2
# THE LAND AND ITS PEOPLE

### The land married to Israel

In Israel, most of the biblical names of places and cities have a meaning, as if God wanted to reveal the genuine identity, character or history of each piece of ground and every city. *Beer Sheba* means seven wells, *Samaria*, or *Shomron* in Hebrew was named so after its former owner *Shemer* (1 Kings 16:24), coming from the root *to keep. Yerushalaim* (Jerusalem) phonetically is a contraction of *peace will be seen twice*, indeed indicating that the Prince of Peace will walk through its gates twice, bringing shalom to its inhabitants. Bethel is God's house and Bethlehem the house of bread. The names of places sometimes relate to the topography of the ground but they often pertain to the people or events of the time. Rehoboth didn't get its name just haphazardly; it comes from the root *rahav* meaning wide, spacious. *Bochim*, meaning *weeping*, is the place where the angel of the Lord rebuked the people of Israel and the Israelites wept (Judges 2:1-5). Throughout the Bible and even today God continues to interact with His people on this piece of land. There He speaks, rebukes, builds, destroys, blesses and even weeps. It is amazing to see how God speaks to men wherever they live, using names of places from this tiny land. In the Bible, the land of the Jews becomes a proxy for God to address issues of the soul but also to bring hope to His children:

*"Then the LORD said to Joshua, 'Today I have rolled away the reproach of Egypt from you.' So the place has been called Gilgal to this day." (Josh. 5:9).*

*Gilgal*, bearing the root *galgal* meaning *wheel* or *legalgel*, means *to roll* and is today the name of a kibbutz.

The personification of the land is such that it is sometimes hard to grasp especially for a Greek mindset. The Bible tells us that "*Jews demand miraculous signs and Greeks look for wisdom*" (1 Corinthians 1:22). This is why it is more natural for somebody with a Hebrew mindset to consider a thought or concept visually, whereas the Greek minded person would dissect it in his mind and analyse it intellectually. God prefers to speak to the Israelites with images that may often strike us as illogical and even preposterous. This is the case when He refers to the land as to a bride:

*"No longer will they call you Deserted, or name **your land** Desolate. But you will be called Hephzibah, and your land Beulah; for the LORD will take delight in you, and **your land will be married**." (Is. 62:4).*

This matter of joining the Jewish people to the land in holy matrimony has far-fetched implications. It confirms God's view of the necessity for His people to have a land and ultimately to settle down on it. It is doubtful that the Jews would still be called a people if they had not been established as a nation on their own land, especially after all the attempts to swallow up Judaism and extinguish it by converting Jews to other religions, mainly Christianity, instead of helping them to discover Yeshua as their Jewish Messiah. It is indeed odd that some Christians deem it logical for any people to have its own land but not for the people of Israel. Consequently Zionism has for many been erased from the Christian lexicon as a concept not politically correct today. It was from the very beginning of the birth of the people of Israel that God associated the idea of the people to its land. This is why, in preparation of His plan, He said to Abram:

*"The LORD had said to Abram, 'Leave your country, your people and your father's household and go **to the land I will show you**'" (Gen. 12:1).*

Abram was supposed to leave His people and his land because he was called to generate a different people and be given another land. In the second verse of Genesis 12 God announced to Abram that he would become a nation. Abraham is not only the father of nations as people often exclusively understand it, but he is also the father of a specific nation through Isaac, the son of the promise and Jacob, the father of the twelve tribes of Israel. He had to be first the father of a particular nation before he became the father of nations but the first is not annulled by the second, otherwise it would make God unfaithful to His own word. Moreover, God does not only value the marriage of the sons of Israel to the land but he extends much further to insinuate a marriage between Himself and His people:

*"As a young man marries a maiden, so will your sons marry you; **as a bridegroom rejoices over his bride, so will your God rejoice over you.**" (Is. 62:5)*

The reason of this joy is this love, so hard to understand, which God shows in the scriptures for His people Israel. How a God, whose primary nature is holiness, can fall in love with a sinful erring people is something that surpasses our comprehension.

Now let us look into the implications of the marriage we see in verses 4 and 5. From Biblical times to the present age it seems that a beautiful love affair has developed between the Jewish people and the land of Israel. In the episode of Jacob who used a stone as a pillow in Bethel, the Jewish sages suggested that Jacob embraced the stone because he knew he was leaving the land. The romance between the land and its people unwinds further on in the scriptures in a delicate and subtle way:

*"Flowers appear on the earth; the season of singing has come, the cooing of doves is heard in **our land**." (S.o.s. 2:12).*

The prophets often react with utter grief at the thought of being separated from the land:

*"The sound of wailing is heard from Zion: 'How ruined we are! How great is our shame! We must leave our land because our houses are in ruins.'" (Jer. 9:19).*

It was God who pronounced the marriage between the sons of Israel and the land called *Beulah*. This word includes the root *master* or also *husband*. Moreover, He declared His joy over this union (Isaiah 62:5) implying His intimate part in it. This love of the land of Israel is profoundly anchored in the Jewish soul to this very day when Jewish children, from tender age, are taught to love and respect the land, to walk on it, to know it and appreciate its beauty, to learn the names of the protected flowers. It is called the Beautiful land (Daniel 8:9; 11:16; 11:41), the land flowing with milk and honey, a land abounding with fruit as it still is today. The attachment of the Israelis to their land has roots going back to biblical times:

> *"Flowers appear on the earth; the season of singing has come, the cooing of doves is heard **in our land** . The fig tree forms its early fruit; the blossoming vines spread their fragrance. Arise, come, my darling; my beautiful one, come with me." (Sos. 2:12-13).*

The rose of Sharon, the slopes and the dew of Mount Hermon, the beauty of Bashan and of Mount Carmel, the gates and walls of Jerusalem are still there for the wanderer to wonder. David goes so far as to bind himself to Jerusalem with an oath:

> *"If I forget you, O Jerusalem, may my right hand forget [its skill]." (Ps. 137:5).*

We need to understand that every Jew embraces these words in his heart and would regard his betrayal of Jerusalem as a curse upon his life. Once in Christ, why would this change, knowing that this is the city on which Yeshua will set His feet to reign?

The fact that the land started to blossom and produce its fruit again after the establishing of the state of Israel and the return of the Jews is not a surprise. Then green patches could be seen in the desert that started to yield its fruits to the nations. Strawberries and flowers are still grown and exported from there to many countries. In Israel it is told that Mount Gilboa, which David cursed after King Saul and his son Jonathan died in battle, remained flowerless until only after 1948 when the Jews returned to their land. This is why, every year during the spring, thousands of Israelis go for excursions on Mount Gilboa to contemplate its flowers. The land responds to its people and the people to the land. In the course of history the land of Israel was occupied by the Medes, the Persians, the Ottomans, the British, and more. Why is it that these peoples could not make the desert blossom? Instead, they left it as a wilderness. However as soon as the Jews returned to their own land, it came to life and gave fruit a hundredfold. From a cultural point of view, once back to the land the Jews started to revive the Hebrew biblical language into modern Hebrew adapted to our time.

Indeed the Jews have a deep love for their land. Can this love vanish? Would the Lord allow this groom to reject her bride forever? If God united the land to her sons, would He contemplate a final separation? Doesn't He hate divorce as He did in ancient times (Malachi 2:16)? Did He change? Never! Certainly, according to a scriptural principle, the land cannot be married to another nation because the Jewish people are still alive today:

*"For example, by law a married woman is bound to her husband as long as he is alive,*

*but if her husband dies, she is released from*
*the law of marriage." (Rom. 7:2).*

God cannot repeal or violate His word. Israel, unlike many ancient peoples, is still in existence and her marriage to the land still stands.

If so, why does He allow temporary separation? The Jewish people was sent into exile to Babylon and some Christian scholars developed the idea that the return of the Jews to the land after 70 years was the last chance that God gave them to settle on it in righteousness. Therefore, they still consider the establishment of Israel in 1948 as an accident of history. The truth is that God's love for the land cannot bear its profanation by its people's sin and the consequence can be separation but never divorce.

**The sin of Israel**

Two things can confuse the mind when trying to find a solution to the Middle East conflict:

- The Jewish separation from the land at different points of history.
- The loss of territory.

The patriarchs knew that the land had been promised to them. Yet on several occasions they were led to leave it. Abraham, fearing starvation, fled to Egypt because of famine (Genesis 12:10), even as he was aware of God's promises to him.

Isaac was warned not to flee but rather to stand his ground on the land:

*"The LORD appeared to Isaac and said,*
*'Do not go down to Egypt ; **live in the land***
***where I tell you to live'"** (Gen. 26:2).*

Abraham and Isaac were supposed to remain in the land according to God's plan. God never intended to uproot them or their descendants. As a matter of fact the Bible is very clear prophetically:

> "My eyes will watch over them for their good, and I will bring them back to this land. I will build them up and not tear them down; I will plant them and **not uproot them**." (Jer. 24:6).

When Joseph required Jacob to leave Canaan and settle in Goshen in Egypt, all of his family went with him:

> Then Jacob left Beersheba, and Israel's sons took their father Jacob and their children and their wives in the carts that Pharaoh had sent to transport him. They also took with them their livestock and the possessions they had acquired in Canaan, and Jacob and all his offspring went to Egypt. He took with him to Egypt his sons and grandsons and his daughters and granddaughters — **all his offspring**. Genesis 46:5-7

And again:

> All those who went to Egypt with Jacob — those who were **his direct descendants**, not counting his sons' wives — numbered sixty-six persons. With the two sons who had been born to Joseph in Egypt, the members of Jacob's family, which went to Egypt, were seventy in all. Genesis 46:26-27

Jacob ran the risk of permanently losing grip on the land of Canaan and this episode might have definitively thwarted the fulfillment of God's promise through him and his offspring. However although all of Jacob's offspring left the land, God showed much later not only that He was able to bring his descendants back, but also that their absence was temporary.

Indeed God, in His unfathomable grace, gave the promises to the patriarchs and in His mercy He allowed erring Israel to dwell in the land despite prevailing sin in her midst. It was never God's intention for the Jews to live on the land only until 70 AD. The Jewish exile following the Romans' invasion of Jerusalem in 70 AD was a temporary correction rather than a final judgment. The evidence came much later when God caused the Jews to return to their land after the Holocaust. This appalling tragedy was surely under God's control and once it was over, the Lord could give back to the Jewish people what they had lost for almost 2000 years: the land. It seems that God had to destroy in order to build afresh, out of the ruins of the Holocaust disaster as a fulfillment of His promise. Some people shrink at the thought that the Holocaust might have fallen upon Israel because of sin, while for others, the Jews had and still have only what they deserve. This is unfortunately what some people still think, animated as they are by a latent anti-Semitic spirit. However, we can only answer this equation in the light of the scriptures. From the flood in Noah's times to Paul who had a thorn in the flesh, we see different expressions of God's discipline. The flood, the Babylonian exile, the loss of parts of the land came without any doubt as a direct consequence of the sin of the people. In Paul's case, one may wonder what the reason for his thorn was. Was it because of his sins or was it to keep him humble?

Perhaps was it because of his election and call that he had to pay such a dear price of suffering? Paul surely had been entrusted with much, therefore he definitely suffered much adversity and went through the furnace of affliction. God has the right to reveal His answers to these questions, but concerning Israel's suffering, it is undeniable that we see a biblical pattern in the cycle of sin and judgment, rebellion and discipline. This pattern leads us to believe that God has not changed the way He deals with His people.

Therefore, the fact that Israel isn't yet settled within the biblical promised borders can be logically and biblically attributed to the sin of the people. But this can only be temporary and although the Jews have no right to claim anything before God, it is out of His immense grace toward a people He loves so passionately, that He holds on to His promise of the land to the end. It is this grace that people can hardly receive. We often think that we need to strive to please God and not to fall short of His standards because if we fail, we would lose His promises, but when God made the promise of the land, it was an unconditional gift. Remember, He made a covenant with Abraham after He put Him to sleep. Then God, as He walked between the pieces of animals, sovereignly pronounced the terms of the covenant:

> *When the sun had set and darkness had fallen, a smoking firepot with a blazing torch appeared and passed between the pieces. On that day the LORD made a covenant with Abram and said, "To your descendants I give this land, from the river of Egypt to the great river, the Euphrates — the land of the Kenites, Kenizzites, Kadmonites,*

*Hittites, Perizzites, Rephaites, Amorites, Canaanites, Girgashites and Jebusites."*
*Genesis 15:17-21*

Abraham was not even given the opportunity to weigh God's terms and agree or reject them. There was no condition attached to the promise and the text does not say that the land wouldn't be given as long as there is sin in Israel, although sin is utterly disgraceful to God and it can cause Him to deprive the people of the land for a time. God made the covenant as a sovereign choice out of pure grace and love. It is this passionate love that we should take into consideration before we intellectually analyze biblical passages concerning Israel and the land. It is God's passionate love for His Old Testament bride which makes any Cartesian dissection of the scriptures inappropriate to comprehend the theme of Israel. It is as if we forcefully wanted to lock this love in the cage of our reasoning and limit God's freedom to act with what belongs to Him in keeping with His own will. Indeed, He often desires to bestow His love and compassion after the longing of His heart:

> *"Don't I have the right to do what I want with my own money? Or are you envious because I am generous?" (Matt. 20:15).*

Yes, *sometimes* God has the right to make an exception to His own rules. In this parable, the Lord's rewards to His workers seem unfair. Some of them have worked longer and harder than others. They probably laboured under the scorching sun while others enjoyed the coolness of the evening, but as unfair as it may look, God's judgments need sometimes to be received in the light of His love for His people. On the other hand, the Jewish people have suffered perhaps more than any other nation on the face of the earth and yet no one would dare accuse God of unfairness. It is hard for a human mind to evaluate and fathom the depth and perfection of God's judgments. Several other biblical instances could be recalled here:

> *"Just as it is written: 'Jacob I loved, but Esau I hated.' What then shall we say? Is God unjust? Not at all! For he says to Moses, 'I will have mercy on whom I have mercy, and I will have compassion on whom I have compassion.'" (Rom. 9:13-15).*

God said this although Jacob stole the blessing from Esau. Joseph gave Benjamin five times what he gave his other brothers although Benjamin was the youngest in the family. Ephraim was privileged over Manasseh and received a better blessing although Manasseh was the eldest.

In the case of His bride Israel, would we really betray the Lord's intended meaning if we rephrased the verse of Matthew 20:15 as follows: "*...or are you envious because I am in love?"* We could say: "*But Lord, aren't you contradicting your own rules? Aren't your ways unchanging and impartial?"* Yet although it is true that His love is equal for all His children, the Lord's answer would remain the same and He is not limited by our logical western reasoning. In the spiritual realm some concepts are foreign to our earthly mindset and both biblical and contemporary history of the Jewish people show us that God has not rejected His bride Israel; this is why Paul exclaims in anticipation of the future: "*Did God reject His people? By no means!" (Romans 11:1).*

Let there be no misunderstanding here: God's word makes it very clear from Genesis to Revelation that He does not have a plan *B* of salvation for the Jews. The gospel claims the same necessity for Jews and non-Jews alike. However, God has His control on the development of events leading to the spiritual restoration of Israel as a nation and His refusal to reject His people ought to be considered as a sovereign act of His unfathomable grace.

In a response to John Piper David Brickner wrote:

> *I agree with you that Israel does not currently enjoy a divine right to the Land. But I would argue that it has never been by divine right but rather by divine mercy that Israel has dwelt in the Land. God blessed Abraham in the land he had promised him though Abraham at times acted in unbelief, at times had to fight for his land, and at one point even paid for his land (and in the end never even possessed all the land that was promised him). Similarly, for much of the biblical record, Israel lived in the land while rebellious and breaking the Mosaic Covenant. Yet God was merciful and allowed Israel to remain in the Land despite her unbelief. He did this because of his gracious promise to Abraham and his descendants. Why could God not act the same in our present-day situation?[3]*

This said, we repeatedly witness how God uses the land to deal with His people. However, God's punishment of the Jews is not always automatic and does not always result in the withdrawal of territories. In the time of Israel's kings who did evil in God's eyes, the people yet remained in the land despite suffering. In fact, the ultimate promise of the land to the chosen people has never been conditional to its behavior. Nevertheless, this does not mean that Israel hasn't paid a high price for her disobedience and God often used the hostility and hatred of her enemies to discipline His people:

*"So I stretched out my hand against you and **reduced your territory**; I gave you over to the greed of your enemies, the daughters of the Philistines, who were shocked by your lewd conduct." (Ezek. 16:27).*

In fact, God allowed the Philistines to encroach on the borders which He had ordained and attributed to Israel. It is as if God retreated from His promise for a while in order to allow His people to adjust to His will and word. In other words, the reduction of territory was used as a rod of correction but was never meant to deprive the people of the land for ever. Israel could not inherit the whole land with its biblical borders while still in sin, but she was allowed to live partially on it and endure correction. Isn't that what we witness today in Israel? This said, a final rejection of Israel from the land would mean God's retreat from His promise. It would also imply His gift of victory to His enemy the devil. This is obviously something that a faithful God cannot conceive.

Yet the cost that Israel generally paid for her sins was often a loss of land, however temporary:

*But if they will confess their sins and the sins of their fathers — their treachery against me and their hostility toward me, which made me hostile toward them so that **I sent them***

*into the land of their enemies — then when their uncircumcised hearts are humbled and they pay for their sin, I will remember my covenant with Jacob and my covenant with Isaac and my covenant with Abraham, and I will remember the land.*
Leviticus 26:40-42

The Lord always remembers His covenant, His promise, His word and He exemplifies it through His people. What good news this is for all of us! In the verses above we need to pay close attention to the order of His covenant this time: first with Jacob, then with Abraham! First His covenant with the twelve tribes of Israel–the Jewish people–then with Abraham, the father of many nations. The goal is always to bless the nations but the plan remains the same and its fulfillment involves His chosen people. This is why Israel cannot be rejected or permanently ousted from the land despite her sin. Nevertheless, correction must come because God cares for His people and disciplines those He loves:

*"For the land will be deserted by them and will enjoy its sabbaths while it lies desolate without them. They will pay for their sins because they rejected my laws and abhorred my decrees." (Lev. 26:43).*

We must be in God's rest in order to be fruitful in His field, but in the same manner, the Lord expects us to give the land rest, as seen above, so that it may produce abundant fruit. It is a matter of sensitivity to and respect for His land. It also confirms that fruit does not come by might or by power and nothing can be deserved but it is already a sign of God's grace which we amply see in the New Covenant.

Above all, the main reason for God's discipline upon Israel is for His own name's sake:

*I dispersed them among the nations, and they were scattered through the countries; I judged them according to their conduct and their actions. And wherever they went among the nations they profaned my holy name, for it was said of them, 'These are the LORD's people, and yet they had to leave his land.' I* **had concern for my holy name**, *which the house of Israel profaned among the nations where they had gone. Ezekiel 36:19-21*

His concern for the glory of His name among the nations is indeed a noble cause and it justifies the loss of territory but it can be only temporary:

*"For I will take you out of the nations; I will gather you from all the countries and* **bring you back into your own land.***" (Ezek. 36:24).*

If God's discipline is temporary, it obviously does in no way annul the promises made to Abraham, Isaac and Jacob. God knew that no nation on the face of the earth was able to live up to His conditions, not even God's people, the Church, so the Lord of all the earth didn't abandon His plan for His people and for His land.

Nevertheless, loss of territory became a recurring pattern in the history of Israel:

*In those days the LORD **began to reduce the size of Israel**. Hazael overpowered the Israelites throughout their territory east of the Jordan in all the land of Gilead (the region of Gad, Reuben and Manasseh), from Aroer by the Arnon Gorge through Gilead to Bashan. 2 Kings 10:32-33*

We see here how the region east of the Jordan River and Bashan (today called the Golan Heights) were punctually amputated from Israel because of sin. In the same way as God reduced the size of the land by bringing enemies and giving them victory over Israel, isn't it logical for him to let Israel recover the land by giving her victory over her enemies? Wouldn't this explain what happened in 1967 when sections of the land were added to the 1948 borders? Then Israel actually returned to part of the Promised Land where David had reigned as king.

However, confession and repentance can obviously abort the exile from the land:

*When your people Israel have been defeated by an enemy because they have sinned against you, and when they turn back to you and confess your name, praying and making supplication to you in this temple, then hear from heaven and forgive the sin of your people Israel and **bring them back to the land you gave to their fathers**. 1 Kings 8:33-34*

Despite God's discipline through exile or the loss of the land, the Israelites had no doubt that the land had

48

been promised for them to ultimately and permanently live on it:

*"then I will let you live in this place, in the land I gave your forefathers **for ever and ever.**" (Jer. 7:7).*

And:

*"O our God, did you not drive out the inhabitants of this land before your people Israel and **give it forever** to the descendants of Abraham your friend?" (2 Chron. 20:7).*

Let there be no mistake: it is before the people of Israel that God drove the enemies and it is to Israel's descendants, not only *Abraham's seed* that the promise of the land was made, as we can see in this verse, but we will come back to this matter further on. After the people pay for the sin committed on the land, God is always gracious toward Israel and His anger is never permanent:

*"Speak tenderly to Jerusalem, and proclaim to her that her hard service has been completed, that her sin has been paid for, that she has received from the LORD's hand double for all her sins." (Is. 40:2).*

Yes, Israel has often paid double for her iniquities. Isn't it written that *"from everyone who has been given much, much will be demanded, and from the one who has been entrusted with much, much more will be asked"?* (Luke 12:48). In the framework of God's correction, the scourge can sometimes look disproportionate but it never denies or cancels the promise that God swore with an oath to Abraham, Isaac and Jacob; as intense as the correction is, so is also the reward:

> *The seed will grow well, the vine will yield its fruit, the ground will produce its crops, and the heavens will drop their dew. I will give all these things as an inheritance to the remnant of this people. As you have been an object of cursing among the nations, O Judah and Israel, so will I save you, and you will be a blessing. Do not be afraid, but let your hands be strong. Zechariah 8:12-13*

It is in the light of all the rebellion and disobedience of Israel that we can measure and start to appreciate God's faithfulness to His word and His munificent grace to all of us.

**Faithfulness to Israel the bride**

Just reading the Lord's hard words against sinning Israel in the scriptures, we might easily conclude that He did not have any choice but to reject her:

> *"'I will punish her for the days she burned incense to the Baals; she decked herself with rings and jewelry, and went after her lovers, but me she forgot,'" declares the LORD. (Hos. 2:13).*

Nevertheless, can He remain angry for long? Look at the next verse:

> *Therefore I am now going to allure her; I will lead her into the desert and speak tenderly to*

50

*her. There I will give her back her vineyards, and will make the Valley of Achor a door of hope. There she will sing as in the days of her youth, as in the day she came up out of Egypt. Hosea 2:14-15*

The reason of His grace and love comes a few verses later through a dramatic declaration:

*"I will betroth you to me **forever**; I will betroth you in righteousness and justice, in love and compassion." (Hos. 2:19).*

We know that the Church is also the bride. In fact, both Israel and the Church are to be seen as the two facets of the same bride who is to become one in Yeshua toward the second coming of Messiah. Already in the Old Testament, much before Yeshua's first coming, the cross and the redemption of the Jewish people, God called Israel His bride. The problem is that many of us cannot conceive two brides. This is where we need a Hebrew minded approach of the text to grasp the concept of two brides as one before God. The Greek mindset has a problem comprehending seemingly paradoxical facets of the same concept. As a result, it has a tendency to choose one at the expense of the other. We often make this error as we try to understand some biblical truths. For instance, Messiah is portrayed both as a Lion and as a Lamb, or as the Everlasting Father and the Son. How can He be a lion and a Lamb, with all the differences implied in this analogy? How can He be both Father and Son (Isaiah 9:6)? On the other hand Yeshua is the only begotten Son but Israel is also called God's Son in Exodus 4:22. How can Yeshua be called the **only** begotten Son of God if there is another son?

This is where we are tempted to choose one truth and reject the second. It is like the Father, the Son and the Holy Ghost. Are they three or one? Difficult to put into words, isn't it? Yet it becomes so easy when grasped in the spirit. In the Old Testament we see the three of them, yet nobody thought in terms of three Gods. It was quite natural to believe that there is a Father, a Son (Psalms 2:12; Isaiah 9:6 etc) and God's spirit. Be that as it may, we generally consider it a paradox to even think of both Israel and the Church as God's bride. Neither Israel nor the Church has come to the degree of perfection demanded by a holy God and although we may think that the Church has a right to be called His bride because of her revelation of Messiah, we can all the same assume that Israel is God's bride in a process of full spiritual restoration. Indeed this process is well under way with the current existence of a Messianic Church and its sanctification.

In fact, these two brides become one as they come together in perfect unity in Him without losing their own respective identity. This perfect unity is a huge leap toward the Millennium when the bride enjoys ineffable joys in the presence of her Lord and Saviour. It is not surprising that the devil is relentlessly in the business of separating the Church from Israel and, if we fall into his trap, this spirit of division and separation can have serious implications as history testifies. In the book of Genesis, God brings Abram to the land and already in chapter 12 we can see a union between this man who came from a quite different country, let alone culture, and this new land. In God's first words to Abraham we can already discern the further promises which will come in the next chapters:

*The LORD had said to Abram, "Leave your country, your people and your father's household and go to the land I will show you. "I will make you into a great nation and I will bless you; I will make your name great, and you will be a blessing. I will bless those who bless you, and whoever curses you I will curse; and all peoples on earth will be blessed through you." Genesis 12:1-3*

Please notice that the word *goy* meaning nation is in the singular in verse 2 in the Hebrew, which confirms that God promised to make him **a** specific great nation and not just *many nations*.

The very fact that God had called Abram to this new land was already secondary to His further promise of the land to him and his descendants:

*"He also said to him, 'I am the LORD, who brought you out of Ur of the Chaldeans **to give you this land to take possession of it.**'" (Gen. 15:7).*

In other words, Abram knew that his blessings depended on the land where he was supposed to settle. He was tested by a famine and decided to separate himself from this land and go to a foreign one, Egypt. This led him from separation to separation: he almost lost his wife by giving her to Pharaoh. Now, some of these Bible stories are often, as the rabbis believe, *signs for our children*, meaning signs for the future, based on the following verse:

*"Here am I, and the children the LORD has given me. **We are signs and symbols** in*

53

*Israel from the LORD Almighty, who dwells on Mount Zion." (Is. 8:18).*

If we interpret the episode of Genesis 12 prophetically, we can see three characters in it: Abraham, Sarah and the land and we can only leave the interpretation to the reader. Could Abraham stand for the people of Israel, Sarah his wife for the land, Pharaoh and Egypt for the nations? Could we apply it to the current situation in the Middle East? What would be God's reaction if the nations usurped the land, as Pharaoh usurped Sarah, separating it from its natural husband Israel? Would this analogy awaken the fear of the Lord among certain Christian circles who advocate the irrelevance of the promise of the biblical land to the Jews. Then we could discern a warning to the nations against separating the land from its people, all the more when we see a further separation, (not a final one, thank God) between Abraham and his wife.

The dissociation of Israel from the land is at the root of the separation between the Church and Israel. In history the Gentiles persecuted the Jews because they were hosted by other nations in countries not their own. This has provoked further suspicion on the Jewish side and the Jews tried everything they could to distance themselves from the non-Jews. Therefore they added laws and Jewish rules which dug even deeper the already existing cultural and religious gap between them and the nations. As a result the Gentiles often reacted with violence, jealousy and hatred. The devil has unfortunately smeared the minds and hearts of both Christians and Jews to build between them a wall of partition which, by God's grace, is gradually crumbling down with the revelation of Yeshua to Israel and the unveiling of Israel in God's plan to the Church.

54

Why is it so hard to see this trend as a gradual process taking place before our eyes today? Please note that the Lord always makes up for the years of barrenness, of patience, of grief with an outburst of joy due to His blessings. Israel has experienced this outburst only partially and yet the Jews are inwardly, perhaps unconsciously longing for the joy of salvation that was promised them as a nation.

Yet the nations and, in a mistaken way, part of the Church today, are denying Israel her right to remain God's bride before and independently of her salvation. This led most of the Christian denominations to the ultimate denial of their Jewish roots. Today secular Israel is tempted by the world to think of herself as just another nation and by the church as merely another mission field. Indeed the pressures of the nations on the Jews to abandon their heritage are tremendous, especially on the secular Jews who begin to doubt God's faithfulness to His promises. This may result in their total abandonment of their ancient faith and may plunge them into the pitfall of humanism where the world is sliding today.

The truth of the matter is that the Church needs the Jews in order for both to become the complete bride that God intends her to be. This is one of the main reasons why Israel is still kept alive and why God is so faithful to her. Unfortunately, the idea that the Church would need Israel to become whole is an offense and a stumbling block to many Christians. Nonetheless, as we will see further on, Israel has still something precious to bring to the Church in the same way as the church has, still today, something utterly essential, Yeshua, the treasure of salvation, to bring to the Jews. It is the duty of the bride, who considers herself more enlightened than unsaved Israel, to give her the best she has and not rebuke, judge or accuse her. Wasn't the revelation which she received for the specific purpose *to make Israel envious* (Romans 11:11)? Now how can the Church achieve this goal if she boasts of having the exclusive monopoly of being God's bride on the ground of her presumed rejection of Israel as the bride she was for Him in Old Testament times? Yet God does with His election according to His will and not to men's logics or political agenda. If He wants to have His two brides at His side with the goal of making them one, what is it to Israel's detractors? It reminds us of Yeshua's words to Peter: *"If I want him to remain alive until I return, what is it to you?"* (John 21:23). Although John was the disciple whom Yeshua loved, it didn't mean in any way that Peter was less cherished or that he was a lesser disciple. Does this mean that God has a dual covenant, one for the Church and another for Israel? Certainly not! Individual salvation needs to be found by faith in Yeshua, but for God, Israel was and remains the same bride who will ultimately be sanctified by faith in the true Jewish Messiah. This is for God a fait accompli as Paul wrote it so long ago, prophesying His people's salvation: *"all Israel will be saved"* (Romans 11:25). This is why the Lord, contemplating Israel as if already at the end of her journey toward complete spiritual restoration, has not deprived her of her title as bride.

Let us now consider for a moment the kind of faithful love which God bestows His bride Israel.

> *Then I passed by and saw you kicking about in your blood, and as you lay there in your blood I said to you, "Live!" I made you grow like a plant of the field. You grew up and developed and became the most beautiful of jewels. Your breasts were formed and your*

*hair grew, you who were naked and bare. Later I passed by, and when I looked at you and saw that you were old enough for love, I spread the corner of my garment over you and covered your nakedness. I gave you my solemn oath and entered into a covenant with you, declares the Sovereign LORD, and you became mine. Ezekiel 16:6-8*

These verses speak of passionate love, admiration and desire but they also reveal how ready God is to covenant with this bride despite the disappointment and jealousy of His heart. Nonetheless, His love for her is not deterred:

*"For the sake of his great name the LORD will not reject his people, because the LORD was pleased to make you His own." (1 Sam.12:22).*

It is astounding that Israel did everything to displease the Lord, yet He never gave up on her. Although she looked for other lovers apart from Him and although she has never had anything on her own credit to attract a holy God, He has not ceased to remain adamant to His covenant with her. If we closely examine the context, we can witness the way He passionately reacts at Israel's sin only to retract from His fury. We see the same pattern throughout the books of the prophets where God not only gives us a historical report in accusation of His people, but He also forecasts the bright and hopeful future of Israel. For instance, sometimes the Lord's anger seems definite and irrevocable:

*"They angered him with their high places; they aroused his jealousy with their idols. When God heard them, he was very angry; **he rejected Israel completely.**"* *(Ps. 78:58-59).*

Let us beware of drawing immature and hasty conclusions from verse 59 for it is balanced, would we dare say, denied, by the following:

*but he chose the tribe of Judah, **Mount Zion, which he loved.** He built his sanctuary like the heights, like the earth that he established forever. He chose David his servant and took him from the sheep pens; from tending the sheep he brought him to be the shepherd **of his people Jacob, of Israel his inheritance.** Psalms 78:68-71*

In the following passage it seems as if God is done with Israel and with the land:

*The word of the LORD came to me: "Son of man, this is what the Sovereign LORD says to the land of Israel: **The end! The end has come upon the four corners of the land. The end is now upon you** and I will unleash my anger against you. I will judge you according to your conduct and repay you for all your detestable practices". Ezekiel 7:1-3*

Weren't her sins immense and didn't He have the right to abort the fulfillment of His promises to her? Yes, but the Lord's hard hand upon Israel has always been for a purpose:

*"I will not look on you with pity or spare you; I will repay you in accordance with your conduct and the detestable practices among you. **Then you will know that it is I the LORD who strikes the blow.**" (Ezek. 7:9).*

The end is never the end of Israel and the purpose is clearly expressed here: *"Then you will know..."*

Even when everything seems lost and the glory departs from the temple in chapter 10, the leaders are judged and exile is decreed in chapter 11, God balances his wrath with the promise that even in the countries where the Jews are dispersed, He *will* be a sanctuary for them (Ezekiel 11:16), He *will* bring them back to their land (verse 17) and He *will* give them an undivided heart (verse 18). It goes on with the condemnation of the false prophets, the sending of famine and sword upon the land in chapter 14, the judgment of Jerusalem in chapter 16 where God promises to reduce Israel's territory in verse 27, but toward the end of the chapter we see God's true heart and plan for the people and for the land He so dearly cherishes:

*This is what the Sovereign LORD says: I will deal with you as you deserve, because you have despised my oath by breaking the covenant. **Yet I will remember the covenant I made with you in the days of your youth, and I will establish an everlasting covenant with you.** Ezekiel 16:59-60*

Notice verse 60, all the above does not in any case invalidate His covenant. This is a principle that we need to keep in mind reading the prophecies concerning erring Israel.

In the book of Hosea, the prophet decrees:

*"Their deeds do not permit them to return to their God. A spirit of prostitution is in their heart; they do not acknowledge the LORD."* *(Hos. 5:4).*

However, in the next chapter God cannot conceal His passionate love and, although this verse is true, albeit the utter extremity of their waywardness, God always leaves an open door for them to return:

**Come, let us return to the LORD.** *He has torn us to pieces but he will heal us; he has injured us but he will bind up our wounds.* **After two days he will revive us; on the third day he will restore us,** *that we may live in his presence. Hosea 6:1-2*

Here repentance appears not only as an exhortation but also as a prophecy which will surely come to pass.
God condemns Israel through the prophet Amos but His conclusion is quite surprising:

*"The days are coming," declares the LORD, "when the reaper will be overtaken by the plowman and the planter by the one treading grapes. New wine will drip from the mountains and flow from all the hills.* **I will bring back my exiled people Israel;** *they will rebuild the ruined cities and live in them. They will plant vineyards and drink their wine; they will make gardens and eat their fruit.* **I will plant Israel in their own land, never again to be uprooted from the land**

*I have given them," says the LORD your
God. Amos 9:13-15*

Yes, *"the Lord has a case against His people, He is
lodging a charge against Israel"* (Micah 6:2b) but Micah
ends up his book with words of comfort and hope:

*You will again have compassion on us;
you will tread our sins underfoot and hurl
all our iniquities into the depths of the sea.
You will be true to Jacob, and show mercy
to Abraham, as you pledged on oath to our
fathers in days long ago. Micah 7:19-20*

Even in times of distress, stimulated by his hope for
the people of Israel, Habakkuk proclaims:

*Though the fig tree does not bud and there
are no grapes on the vines, though the olive
crop fails and the fields produce no food,
though there are no sheep in the pen and
no cattle in the stalls, yet I will rejoice in the
LORD, I will be joyful in God my Savior.
Habakkuk 3:17-18*

Zephaniah joins the procession to warn Judah with
the Lord's warning:

*"I will stretch out my hand against Judah and
against all who live in Jerusalem. I will cut
off from this place every remnant of Baal,
the names of the pagan and the idolatrous
priests" (Zeph. 1:4).*

However, God's promise to return the Jews to their land doesn't tarry under the prophet's pen:

> *"'At that time I will gather you; at that time I will bring you home. I will give you honor and praise among all the peoples of the earth when I restore your fortunes before your very eyes,' says the LORD." (Zeph. 3:20).*

Israel's history is marked with countless episodes in which God expressed His fierce anger at the Jewish people but He never predicted the land to any other nation. On the other hand, the Bible is very clear concerning the enemies of the Jews.

Obadiah exclaims in prophecy:

> *"Your warriors, O Teman, will be terrified, and everyone in Esau's mountains will be cut down in the slaughter. Because of the violence against your brother Jacob, you will be covered with shame; you will be destroyed forever." (Ob. 9-10).*

How relevant these verses sound after 2000 years of persecution of the Jews! Besides Esau remained animated by hatred toward the children of Israel for his whole life and he failed to understand God's plan for the land through his brother Jacob. It was out of defiance to God and to his brother that he chose to go to Seir while Jacob chose to settle in Succoth. Then Esau and his descendants embraced a basic enmity to God's people. Esau was actually the only man who attracted God's repulsion to the point of hatred. The fact that Paul mentions this particular hatred under the New Covenant means that, beyond the man, it was the spirit in action that God hated. Esau's descendants were the Edomites, the people of Mount Seir who sought to possess the land of Israel contrary to the Lord's will:

> *Because you harbored an ancient hostility and delivered the Israelites over to the sword at the time of their calamity, the time their punishment reached its climax, therefore as surely as I live, declares the Sovereign LORD, I will give you over to bloodshed and it will pursue you. Since you did not hate bloodshed, bloodshed will pursue you. I will make Mount Seir a desolate waste and cut off from it all who come and go. Ezekiel 35:5-8*

Is there any people doing violence to Israel today? Certainly so! But what can we say about all the prophecies of destruction of her enemies? Weren't they fulfilled? Absolutely! Where are the Canaanites, the Girgashites, the Hitites, the Amorites, the Jebusites, the Perizzites, the Hivites? What has become of the powerful Babylonians, the Persian Empire, the Medes, the Egyptian civilization? How have the Romans fallen from their pinnacle of glory? What remains of the Greek empire or the British Commonwealth? The list is long, but even after 2000 years of persecution, suffering and shame, Israel is back upon this good old land and it is not an accident of history, since the Jews govern it today, as David and the Jewish kings did back in ancient times. God's faithfulness to Israel is exemplary, sobering and perhaps something which should provoke awe instead of jealousy and anger. Even in prophecy the apostle Paul doesn't leave any doubt:

*What advantage, then, is there in being a Jew, or what value is there in circumcision? Much in every way! First of all, they have been entrusted with the very words of God. What if some did not have faith?* **Will their lack of faith nullify God's faithfulness?** *Not at all! Let God be true, and every man a liar. As it is written: "So that you may be proved right when you speak and prevail when you judge." Romans 3:1-4*

God's faithfulness is not limited to a single punctual fulfillment of a prophecy but it repeats across history. Thus Jeremiah's repeated prophecies of the Jews' return to the land were not necessarily completely fulfilled at their return from the Babylonian exile, especially when we know that they were uprooted again in 70 AD. The Bible tells us specifically that they would not be uprooted again (Amos 9:15). So whether the world likes it or not, the Jews are biblically supposed to settle in Israel for good. In the light of this truth, it is difficult to dwarf the existence of the state of Israel and not recognize it as a fulfillment of God's faithful promise. Yes, as much as it may displease many people, the Jewish people are in the Middle East to stay! In fact, had the Lord fail to remain faithful to His promises to Israel, it would be a real flaw in His character and would put a big question mark on His faithfulness to the Church.

## Chapter 3
# THE PROMISE OF THE LAND

### The earthly and heavenly counterparts

T he promise of the land is dual: it is both earthly and heavenly. This is the principle of the dual counterparts seen in the Bible. The Lord promised us an eternal dwelling, a perfect abode in the New Jerusalem but His heart is also to see men prosper upon His land on earth to the fulfillment of His goal.

From the beginning, God worked through man according to heavenly patterns:

> *"They serve at a sanctuary that is **a copy and shadow of what is in heaven**. This is why Moses was warned when he was about to build the tabernacle: 'See to it that you make everything **according to the pattern shown you on the mountain.'" (Heb. 8:5).***

Apparently there was a sanctuary in heaven and the Lord wanted Moses to build its earthly counterpart which had to be identical to the one seen in the heavenly realms. It must have been awesome for Moses to see the heavens open and gaze at the transcendent sublimity of the heavenly sanctuary. Yet for many centuries the earthly counterpart remained parallel to its perfect pattern in heavens.

We saw this principle earlier in the scriptures:

*"Nevertheless, death reigned from the time of Adam to the time of Moses, even over those who did not sin by breaking a command, as did Adam, **who was a pattern of the one to come**." (Rom. 5:14).*

As a matter of fact, in this case the earthly counterpart was meant to be as identical as possible to its perfect pattern, Yeshua:

*Then God said, "Let us make man **in our image, in our likeness**, and let them rule over the fish of the sea and the birds of the air, over the livestock, over all the earth, and over all the creatures that move along the ground." So God created man in his own image, **in the image of God he created him**; male and female he created them. Genesis 1:26-27*

However, although Yeshua was the perfect Adam, God didn't remove man from the earth at the incarnation of His Son but He left man for a purpose: we are supposed to be gradually transformed into His likeness:

*"And we, who with unveiled faces all reflect the Lord's glory, are **being transformed into his likeness with ever-increasing glory**, which comes from the Lord, who is the Spirit." (2 Cor. 3:18).*

This is again a clear evidence of God's patience and grace. He is patient with His creation and contributes to its improvement from glory to glory and from holiness to holiness. He also wants to reveal His infinite power and greatness by choosing to work out perfectness from an imperfect creation. This is often so difficult for the human mind to grasp especially when man tries to spiritualize everything. Consequently, there is a tendency to build a doctrine that eliminates much of God's earthly plan by spiritualizing the promises made to Israel and to see them inherited by the Church.

Similarly, we are all aware that there are two Jerusalem and the one we know in the Middle East is only an earthly counterpart, a poor reflection of its pattern in heavens. The Bible clearly shows that Jerusalem has an umbilical cord attached to heavens and is God's chosen place on earth:

> *He said: "Son of man, this is the place of* ***my throne and the place for the soles of*** ***my feet****. This is where I will live among the Israelites forever. The house of Israel will never again defile my holy name — neither they nor their kings — by their prostitution and the lifeless idols of their kings at their high places". Ezekiel 43:7*

This is His chosen holy place about which He prophesied that the children of Israel would never again defile His holy name. Even if we believe that the restoration of the physical borders, as prophesied in Ezekiel 47 is for the Millennium, it is still something that ought to be expected on earth. During the Millennium Yeshua's presence will reverberate from Jerusalem to the rest of

Israel and unto the nations. This is how we understand the importance of a land where He will reign.

> *"On that day his feet will stand on the Mount of Olives, east of Jerusalem, and the Mount of Olives will be split in two from east to west, forming a great valley, with half of the mountain moving north and half moving south." (Zech. 14:4).*

He will be declared king over the very spot which has been greatly coveted by the devil, so it is very significant for our Messiah to affirm His sovereignty, not just in heaven but also on the earth. We get a glimpse of the importance of Jerusalem not only in history but eternally in the following passage:

> *How good and pleasant it is when brothers live together in unity! It is like precious oil poured on the head, running **down** on the beard, running **down** on Aaron's beard, **down** upon the collar of his robes. It is as if the dew of Hermon were falling **on Mount Zion. For there the LORD bestows his blessing, even life forevermore.** Psalms 133:1-3*

First we see the motion of the blessing. Through the outpouring of the oil, the Holy Spirit comes down to earth with the names of real earthly locations in Israel. Then we see the climax of this blessing in Jerusalem, not the heavenly but the earthly, forevermore.

According to the rabbinical Scriptures, in the desert the camp of Israel had three degrees of sanctity: First the inner sanctuary where the divine presence would manifest, second the camp of the Levites and then the camp of the Israelites.[4]

It is therefore not far-fetched to imagine that in the Millennium, Jerusalem will be the holiest spot because of the Lord's presence:

> *"The moon will be abashed, the sun ashamed; **for the LORD Almighty will reign on Mount Zion and in Jerusalem**, and before its elders, gloriously." (Is. 24:23).*

This is why the enemy's attacks against this city have been so ruthless. Let us check some biblical information concerning the Millennium in order to avoid any misunderstanding. According to Revelation 20, the order of events is as follows:

- The first resurrection.
- The saints reign with Him for a thousand years.
- Satan is released for a time to deceive the nations.
- The battle of Gog and Magog confirms that the enemy will concentrate his last fight against Jerusalem (Revelation 20:9) on earth.
- The devil is finally thrown to the lake of burning sulfur.
- The new heavens and new earth appear.
- The New Jerusalem descends.

Therefore the nations exist on earth during the reign of the Lord for a thousand years. The Millenium does not take place on the new earth but on the same planet on which we live today according to the sequence of events. Although we do not have much biblical information on the Millenium, we recognize that Yeshua will reign on the earth for a thousand years.

Nonetheless the book of Isaiah seems to give us some hints pertaining to the thousand years which indicate their fulfillment on earth:

> *The wolf will live with the lamb, the leopard will lie down with the goat, the calf and the lion and the yearling together; and a little child will lead them. The cow will feed with the bear, their young will lie down together, and the lion will eat straw like the ox. The infant will play near the hole of the cobra, and the young child put his hand into the viper's nest. They will neither harm nor destroy on all my holy mountain, for* **the earth** *will be full of the knowledge of the LORD as the waters cover the sea. Isaiah 11:6-9*

We can securely conclude that the nations will still be in their own territory and so will Israel, only with its biblical borders because Ezekiel 47 has to be fulfilled on earth. Israel and Jerusalem with the third temple at its center will be there to exemplify the communion that Yeshua desires with God's children. This is why He has sent an instruction to the nations to go up to Jerusalem and present themselves before Him year after year (Zechariah 14:16). The Bible does not hide that there are several degrees of sanctity in His kingdom. Some will be doorkeepers in the house of the Lord (Psalms 84:10) while others will sit with Him on His throne (Revelation 3:21). Without making a theology or a dogma out of this, it seems that the Millennium may be a transition period when man is encouraged to seek God's proximity, both physically and spiritually for 1000 years, before he can inherit not only the kingdom but also God's eternal presence in the New Jerusalem. It will be a progression to enable the Lord's bride to enter the New Jerusalem according to His perfect will and Yeshua's victory on the earth is therefore symbolically very important. The devil is the prince of this world (John 14:30) and he plays havoc in the nations. Indeed he will even be allowed to stir rebellion in mankind toward the end of the Millennium, but a time is coming when he is overthrown and then he will not have any influence on the earth any longer. Then the Messiah will pronounce Himself king over the world for the blessing of God's children. This is why the Lord has always spoken of His advent down on earth whereas many Christians generally mainly think of believers going up to heavens. His will needs to be done on earth as it is in heavens. The Lord Himself visited the earth several times as shown in the Scriptures. He came to be born on the earth and promised His return with His saints to the earth to reign in the messianic era for 1000 years. It is only after He assumes His complete triumph and dominion over the earth that the new earth and the new heavens are created and the New Jerusalem comes down from heavens. So we understand that the promise of the land to the Jews (the 12 tribes of Israel) with its biblical borders and Jerusalem as capital needs to be fulfilled on earth before or at the very start of the Millennium.

The earthly city is far from being what we all expect and it certainly falls short of God's glory. Nevertheless, God has been exceedingly patient with the city of the Great King. Everyone who walks in its streets and gazes at its ramparts cannot but sense the overwhelming hope that this city inspires, even in its present precarious state.

Yet according to the same principle, God is not content to have a heavenly kingdom but He desires to install His sovereignty upon the earth and specifically from a piece of land called Israel. So again, we have a kingdom in heavens and its counterpart on earth. This is one of the main reasons why God has His eyes continually upon imperfect Israel (Deuteronomy 11:12). He is patient with Israel but not the less eager to see this land as the bedrock of blessings for the whole world:

*"May the LORD bless you from Zion all the days of your life; may you see the prosperity of Jerusalem," (Ps. 128:5).*

Although God's kingdom in heavens remains intact, He doesn't do away with its earthly counterpart in the Middle East and He is determined to unfold His plan completely on and from the land of Israel. This way we can see that the spiritual and the physical are linked together. They stand in parallel until the time when God dissolves the elements and creates new heavens and a new earth, but despite men's conflicting doctrines, we are not there yet and the Lord loves to work out His plan through an imperfect mankind and a profaned land in the Middle East. This is how we can understand the progression from our present era, the Millennium and the final destination in the New Jerusalem. As a matter of fact, during the thousand years of Yeshua's kingdom on earth, the nations will still be tested toward the end of that period but only those who will pass the test successfully and prove themselves faithful to their Lord will step into the perfect abode He has reserved for them in the New Jerusalem. Yet we clearly understand from the scriptures that Yeshua will reign from earthly Jerusalem and that Israel will still be a land in the Middle East with extended borders exactly according to His covenant with Abraham. So it is not surprising that God's plan concerning the land is being progressively unfolded, the borders progressively recovered and His people progressively saved until the complete salvation of the nation and its full union with the Church remnant.

The link between the heavenly and its earthly counterpart is exemplified in the passage of what is generally called *Jacob's ladder.*

*When he reached a certain place, he stopped for the night because the sun had set. **Taking one of the stones there**, he put it under his head and lay down to sleep. He had a dream in which he saw **a stairway resting on the earth, with its top reaching to heaven**, and the angels of God were ascending and descending on it. Genesis 28:11-12*

In verse 12 the angels were linking heavens and earth and specifically that part of the earth which Jacob called *Beth El.* It was like a prophetic umbilical cord between heavens and earth, heralding the future messianic era when Yeshua comes back from heavens to set His kingdom on the earth from Jerusalem for a thousand years. We can only understand the implication of this passage in the light of God's reiteration of the promise of the land to Jacob from Bet El (Genesis 28:13).

In other words, this land has been, is and will be used by God to show His ability to turn the earthly counterpart into perfection. He has always desired to make it the centre of His messianic kingdom and this is why the devil is so enraged against it, attacking it from all sides. This is also why he inspires the nations and induces them to such an enmity toward Israel. His tactic is basically to blur the minds and twist the truth even to deceive the saints. God has chosen the Jewish people to carry out His vision upon this piece of land;

73

as a result, the Jews will remain the focus of the devil's fury. Therefore in order to achieve his goal, Satan minimizes the importance of the land of Israel in such a humanistic way that it becomes appealing to many believers in Christ. He will not bother for them to focus on the heavenly kingdom as long as their attention is diverted from its earthly counterpart and from what he tries to achieve upon it through his evil schemes. Yet the Lord had warned the nations against any attack on His people, revealing His close connection to Israel:

> *"For this is what the LORD Almighty says: 'After he has honored me and has sent me against the nations that have plundered you — for whoever touches you touches the apple of his eye'" (Zech. 2:8).*

May the nations take this solemn oath seriously and position themselves accordingly to be participants of God's unfolding plan upon the land of Israel in these end times.

### To Abraham, Isaac and Jacob

> *"I will make you into **a great nation** and I will bless you; I will make your name great, and you will be a blessing. I will bless those who bless you, and whoever curses you I will curse; and all peoples on earth will be blessed through you." (Gen. 12:2-3).*

When God first spoke to Abram, before making him the father of many nations, He promised to make him a great nation and He meant the nation of Israel as we can understand in verse 3: *"will bless those who bless you..."* which is repeated further on by Balaam:

> *"Like a lion they crouch and lie down, like a lioness — who dares to rouse them? 'May those who bless you be blessed and those who curse you be cursed!'" (Num. 24:9).*

Balaam does not have any doubt about the identity of the people to be blessed. He prophesied each time about the people of Israel as he took a different look at it from diverse angles.

Abraham insisted that his son Isaac would not leave the land even to get a wife:

> *"**Make sure that you do not take my son back there**," Abraham said. "The LORD, the God of heaven, who brought me out of my father's household and my native land **and who spoke to me and promised me on oath, saying, 'To your offspring I will give this land' — he will send his angel before you so that you can get a wife for my son from there".** Genesis 24:6-7*

Please notice how Abraham makes the connection between his insistence not to uproot Isaac from the land in verse 6 and the promise of the land in verse 7. He was certain that God would not only provide a wife for Isaac but would also lead her to come to Isaac and not the other way around. The whole chapter (Genesis 24) shows at length how the Lord's hand was upon Abraham's servant to guide the course of events. It was Rebecca's coming to Isaac and not Isaac's coming to Rebecca that was ordained and inspired by God.

Abraham wanted to make sure that Isaac remained in the land at least until he truly and fully received the assurance of his inheritance on it through the matrimony of Isaac and Rebecca, knowing that he would become not just many *nations* in Christ but *a specific nation* settled on its own land.

Besides, we see God's similar admonishment to Jacob:

> *"And the LORD said unto Jacob, Return unto the land of thy fathers, and to thy kindred; and I will be with thee." (Gen. 31:3).*

In his prayer, as he saw himself in danger, Jacob reminded God of His promise, knowing that his posterity was at stake:

> *"Then Jacob prayed, 'O God of my father Abraham, God of my father Isaac, O LORD, who said to me, 'Go back to your country and your relatives, and I will make you prosper,'" (Gen. 32:9).*

Not only his posterity was in danger but he also ran the risk of losing grip of the inheritance of the land which God had promised through him to his descendants already in his loins:

> *"Save me, I pray, from the hand of my brother Esau, for I am afraid he will come and attack me, **and also the mothers with their children.**" (Gen. 32:11).*

Jacob was very much aware of the fact that this land was destined to the posterity coming from him.

Nevertheless it could be argued that the promises made to the Patriarchs were to be fulfilled only in Christ but we cannot ignore the unconditional character of the promises made to Abraham as Chuck Cohen wrote:

*Since this multifaceted promise to Abraham is unconditional and indivisible, if one no longer believes the land of Israel is promised to the Jewish people, then one can no longer believe the gospel promises either and therefore must believe all of us will simply perish forever. But the promise of the land remains valid and Yeshua still reveals Himself to the Jews and the gentiles everywhere.*[5]

God never conditioned the promise of the land to the salvation of His people. Besides, we saw the promise of the land to Israel fulfilled already in history independently from the salvation of the Jews, and this is all the more true today as the Jews are back to their land. One of the passages of scriptures usually advanced by the adepts of "fulfillment theology" is the following:

*"The promises were spoken to Abraham and to his seed. The Scripture does not say 'and to seeds,' meaning many people, but 'and to your seed,' meaning one person, who is Christ." (Gal. 3:16).*

This is a pertinent point concerning salvation. However, in this verse the apostle Paul wrote of God's promises made to Abraham's seed, stressing that the word is in its singular form, meaning Christ. He meant that the inheritance of God's kingdom depended by faith on *the seed* which is Messiah and not on the observance of the law which was given 400 years later after the promise made to Abraham. So Paul focused here on the spiritual counterpart of the land, God's kingdom. Yet in the previous verse (Galatians 3:15) Paul established a principle: one covenant cannot be set aside at the expense of the other. It means that the covenants are fulfilled but not disposed of. So the promises to the patriarchs remain valid. They just need to be understood in their respective fulfillment, this is why it is interesting to see how the same promises are repeated to Abraham's son and to Jacob.

When the promises are confirmed to Isaac (Genesis 26:3-4) we also see the singular form of the word "seed", which leads us to understand what Paul emphasized as the spiritual facet of the promise. Isaac understood the physical earthly dimension of the promise by making it clear to Jacob that his descendants were not supposed to remain aliens in the land but to possess it:

> *"May he give you and your descendants the blessing given to Abraham, so **that you may take possession of the land** where you now live as an alien, **the land God gave to Abraham.**" (Gen. 28:4).*

Moreover, when the promise of the land was confirmed to Jacob, the father of the 12 tribes of Israel, the word *seed* in Hebrew becomes both singular and plural (*seeds* or *descendants*). For instance:

> *"The land I gave to Abraham and Isaac I also give to you, and I will give this land to your **descendants** after you." (Gen. 35:12).*

Here again the word *descendants* or *seed* is in the singular form in Hebrew, so the verse confirms what Paul meant in Galatians 3:16 where he was focusing on the promises to Abraham's seed, meaning Messiah Yeshua. However, it was only one facet of the prophecy and the other facet is seen in the following verse describing God's promise to Jacob:

> *"There above it stood the LORD, and he said: 'I am the LORD, the God of your father Abraham and the God of Isaac. I will give you and **your descendants** the land on which you are lying.'" (Gen. 28:13).*

Here the singular form has switched to plural in Hebrew, pointing at the descendants inheriting the promised portion of land on the earthly counterpart, the land of Israel, and not only the spiritual. Here the land was specifically promised to the people of Israel, descendants of Jacob through his twelve sons and, as though to dissipate any misunderstanding, the text refers to a specific physical land, stipulating *the land on which you are lying* and not a spiritual entity somewhere in heavens. Besides God had led Abraham to actually see the land which was promised to his descendants so that he may really believe and understand the physical nature of the promise:

> *"The LORD said to Abram after Lot had parted from him, '**Lift up your eyes from where you are and look north and south, east and west**. All the land that you see I will give to you and your offspring **forever.**'" (Gen. 13:14-15).*

The promises made by God to the patriarchs were confirmed by Messiah Yeshua Himself according to Paul's commentary:

*For I tell you that Christ has become **a servant of the Jews** on behalf of God's truth, **to confirm the promises made to the patriarchs** so that the Gentiles may glorify God for his mercy, as it is written: "Therefore I will praise you among the Gentiles; I will sing hymns to your name." Romans 15:7-9*

Paul was fully aware that the promise of the land was included in verse 8. So in Galatians 3:16 Paul makes a point on the paramount importance of the ultimate promise of salvation by faith in Yeshua, which is conspicuously more precious to the Lord than all the dwellings of Jacob on earth:

*"The LORD loves the gates of Zion more than all the dwellings of Jacob." (Ps. 87:2)*

Here we can see the spiritual meaning of Zion, the New Jerusalem. However, it doesn't mean that God cancels His promise concerning the dwellings of Jacob on the land of Israel. The promise of the New Jerusalem for the believers and the promise of a physical land in the Middle East stand side by side and are very relevant in the end times although they succeed in sequence.

Besides, when Rebecca was pregnant with her twins who were literally smashing each other in her womb according to the original Hebrew, she went to enquire of the Lord who answered:

*"The LORD said to her, '**Two nations** are in your womb, and two peoples from within you will be separated; one people will be stronger than the other, and the older will serve the younger.'" (Gen. 25:23).*

Jacob was referred to as *a* nation and not many nations. By the way, the fact that the older would serve the younger does not necessarily mean that he would have to suffer from this condition. It was God's plan for the welfare of both of them. Serving is not a bad word in God's lexicon. Sometimes we are called to serve and a nation may be called to serve another nation at different stages of its history. Didn't Israel serve many nations in the past? However, this was the way that God chose to discipline His people in order to help it grow stronger and wiser. Today, although the Palestinians don't have sovereignty over the land, it would be objectively improper to conclude that they are serving the Israelis in a way indicating some kind of bondage. Although there may be some Israeli oppression to some degree, they can expect the Lord's blessing upon them even in the present situation as they trust in His perfect plan:

*"Every man will sit under his own vine and under his own fig tree, and no one will make them afraid, for the LORD Almighty has spoken." (Mic. 4:4).*

Again, the fact that the promise made to Abraham has a spiritual dimension does not exclude its physical counterpart, the promise of the land to God's people. On the other hand, He has a plan for the Palestinians without altering His promises to Israel.

## The validity of the land in prophecy

Some theologians believe that the land has lost its importance since Israel has been replaced by the Church because of the Jews' supposed stubbornness in rejecting Jesus. This interpretation of the Scriptures only strengthened the opinion of those who claim that the promises given by God to Israel are now inherited by the Church. This theology is caused by an inability to conciliate Old and New Testament. Marcion, one of the first fathers of the church used to see the New Testament superior to the Old. This idea has remained deeply inlaid in a large section of Christian theology which has a tendency to see some verses of the New Testament contradict other verses of the Old. As a result, their conclusions implicitly insinuate that God made some mistakes in the Old Testament but corrected them in an updated version called the New Testament. This kind of mindset automatically discards all the Old Testament prophecies for and through Israel. With such an erroneous understanding of the scriptures, some passages of the New Testament find themselves in direct contradiction with other verses from the Old. For instance in the episode of the encounter between Yeshua and the Samaritan woman, she asks Him a question:

*"Our fathers worshiped on this mountain, but you Jews claim that the place where we must worship is in Jerusalem." (John 4:20).*

She based her assumption on what she knew from the Jewish tradition and what she heard about the Torah:

*"Three times a year all your men are to appear before the Sovereign LORD, the God of Israel." (Ex. 34:23).*

Yeshua's answer may seem to change the commandment entirely:

*Jesus declared, "Believe me, woman, a time is coming when you will worship the Father **neither on this mountain nor in Jerusalem.** You Samaritans worship what you do not know; we worship what we do know, for salvation is from the Jews. Yet a time is coming and has now come when the true worshipers will worship the Father in spirit and truth, for they are the kind of worshipers the Father seeks. **God is spirit, and his worshipers must worship in spirit and in truth." John 4:21-24***

Yeshua meant that we will not have to seek God's presence in Jerusalem as our forefathers did in the Old Testament because the Lord will be available everywhere by His spirit. Nonetheless, this does not in any way cancel His prophecies of the establishment of the land and the settlement of the Jews on it. Neither does it cancel the Old Testament prophecies concerning worship in the holy land as we see it confirmed in the book of Zechariah. There God clearly commands the nations to come to Jerusalem once a year at the Feast of Tabernacles:

*Then the survivors from all the nations that have attacked Jerusalem will go up year after year to worship the King, the LORD*

*Almighty, and to celebrate the Feast of Tabernacles . If any of the peoples of the earth do not go up to Jerusalem to worship the King, the LORD Almighty, they will have no rain. Zechariah 14:16-17*

There is no doubt that this prophecy has not yet been fulfilled: all the nations have not yet attacked Jerusalem, they have not yet come every year to Jerusalem at the Feast of Tabernacles and have not been destroyed by God, as seen in verse 12 and in Zechariah 12:9. This is even more so as we realize that the context of Zechariah 14 refers to the end times, just before Yeshua's second coming. So although in John 4 Yeshua speaks of the omnipresence of the Holy Spirit and the freedom of access into the spiritual holy of holies for the true worshippers, both prophecies in Zechariah 14 and in John 4 remain valid and one does not exclude the other. This is where we see that the Old Testament and the New are a whole entity and should be grasped as such. While it is true that *when there is a change of the priesthood there must also be a change of the law* (Hebrews 7:12), God established in the Torah and the prophets some truths whose immovability need to be discerned in the spirit. Even in the Torah there are still some commandments which we, as believers in Yeshua, naturally observe.

In the same way, the Old Testament prophecies are a beacon and sometimes a warning especially when they apply to Israel in the end times. Israel is indeed the prophetic clock of the Church and Christians would do well to pay more attention to it. Many of these prophecies pertaining to the land are actually occurring in the Middle East conflict in which the land represents the core of the dilemma. It is inappropriate to automatically spiritualize the Old Testament and disconnect it from the reality on the ground: In this respect Ulf Ekman wrote:

> *God is a God of history: He has decided to operate through history, geography and statistics, in other words with people, places and facts. Other religions ignore facts, focusing instead on fable and fantasy. But the God of Israel is the Truth and He deals with realities.*[6]

Confusing the Mosaic covenant and the rest of the Old Testament is another common mistake. While part of the Mosaic covenant is obsolete because we are in a new and better dispensation, the prophecies seen in the rest of the scriptures are nonetheless valid in our faith and theology. Here is a vivid example relative to the land:

> *But you, O mountains of Israel, will produce branches and fruit for **my people Israel, for they will soon come home.** I am concerned for you and will look on you with favor; you will be plowed and sown, and I will multiply the number of people upon you, even the whole house of Israel. The towns will be inhabited and the ruins rebuilt. I will increase the number of men and animals upon you, and they will be fruitful and become numerous. I will settle people on you as in the past and will make you prosper more than before. Then you will know that I am the LORD. I will cause people, my people Israel, to walk upon you. **They will possess you**, and you will be their inheritance; **you***

**will never again deprive them of their children.** *Ezekiel 36:8-12*

As we have seen above, this prophecy cannot refer to the return of Babylon since the Jews were exiled again in 70 AD and the end of verse 12 would not apply. Even if this passage is understood to pertain to life in the Millennium, it doesn't deny reality on the ground today when practically every part of this prophecy is fulfilled in Israel.

Even the veracity of the fulfillment of the prophecies in Christ was always seen in parallel with their physical fulfillment. The way Zacharias receives the new born Messiah is very revealing of the awareness which the Jews had, 2000 years ago, of God's plan for the holy land:

> *His father Zechariah was **filled with the Holy Spirit and prophesied:** "Praise be to the Lord, the God of Israel, because he has come and has **redeemed his people.** He has raised up a horn of salvation for us in the house of his servant David (as he said through his holy prophets of long ago), **salvation from our enemies and from the hand of all who hate us** — to show mercy to our fathers and to remember his holy covenant, **the oath he swore to our father Abraham: to rescue us from the hand of our enemies,** and to enable us to serve him without fear." Luke 1:67-74*

First in verse 68 Zacharias foresaw the redemption of God's people and there isn't any doubt that he referred to the Jewish people, "*adding the house of His servant David"* (verse 69). Then he linked the coming of Messiah to the riddance of the enemies of Israel (verse 71). Here we might think that Zacharias, like the Jews of that time, was waiting for a hero who would physically defeat the enemies of Israel, but verse 67 confirms that he was prophesying under the inspiration of the Holy Spirit and not expressing his own opinion. By the same spirit he implicitly declared that the nature of God's oath made to Abraham was not only spiritual but also physical (verses 73 & 74). It mentioned not only Yeshua's defeat over our spiritual enemy, the devil, but also over Israel's physical enemies, explicitly those who seek to confiscate the land. At last, this led him to profess the ultimate goal assigned to the Jewish people: *"to enable us to serve Him without fear"*. Zacharias knew in his spirit that the enemies of Israel would not vanish overnight. He apparently had a revelation not only of the spiritual but also of the physical battle over Israel on the ground both in his time and in the future.

Nevertheless, some theologians would argue that there is no scriptural basis anymore for a Jewish State in the Middle East. By that they mean that Joshua's conquest over the land was ordained by God but it was only for a season. Yet Joshua obeyed God in his conquests to give the future inheritance of the land to the people of Israel according to God's own command:

> *No Anakites were left in Israelite territory; only in Gaza, Gath and Ashdod did any survive. So Joshua took **the entire land**, just as the LORD had directed Moses, and he gave it as an **inheritance to Israel** according to their tribal divisions. Then the land had rest from war. Joshua 11:22-23*

In fact, Joshua did not conquer the whole land as God had planned (Joshua 13:1) but he spared some Gentile peoples who became *thorns and briers* in the Israelites' eyes. After Joshua, nowhere in the Bible did God say that the Israelites should permanently withdraw from these territories. Their retreat from the land in the course of history was only for a season and was allowed by the Lord because of sin as we have seen above. The evidence is that God did not only give the land to Joshua in his battles but He also prophesied it to the Jewish people:

> *This is what the Sovereign LORD says: "These are the boundaries by which you are to divide **the land for an inheritance among the twelve tribes of Israel**, with two portions for Joseph. You are to divide it equally among them. Because I swore with uplifted hand to give it to your forefathers, this land will become your inheritance."*
> *Ezekiel 47:13-14*

The whole chapter is prophetic and here the Lord is unequivocal about his attribution of the land to Israel: it will be distributed to the people of Israel, and this time, the expression *the twelve tribes of Israel* does not leave any doubt but specifically describes the Jewish people. It unveils God's long-term vision.

In the light of this passage, some Christians would agree to allow the Jews to live in their land as a nation but would limit them to some internationally recognized borders. This option is very tempting as it seeks a consensus which, by trying to please everyone, would reach some sort of compromise. In fact this reflects another problem in the interpretation of Old Testament prophecies; times are changing as well as the culture and mindset of civilizations. Concepts that were logical centuries ago may sound almost unacceptable nowadays and modern thinking would treat ancient values as archaic and even inhuman. This is why the word of God often repeats the word *remember* in the scriptures and He remains the same yesterday, today and forever. The Israelites had often forgotten, sometimes even knowingly set aside commandments and precepts from ancient times and they paid dearly for it. God had to remind them as He still does today:

*"This is what the LORD says: 'Stand at the crossroads and look; **ask for the ancient paths**, ask where the good way is, and walk in it, and you will find rest for your souls. **But you said, 'We will not walk in it.'"** (Jer.6:16).*

Today one of the main controversies between secular and religious Jews is whether or not to adapt to the values and the trends of our age. The secular Jews often give practices from other nations as examples to follow, knowing they are contradictory to some biblical principles, even running the risk of bringing a curse upon the land and the people. In the same way the nations and even a majority of believers in Yeshua find all kinds of excuses to treat the Old Testament as obsolete or to twist the meaning of some Old Testament passages in order to adapt them to a modern mindset and make them more acceptable. This is often how the prophecies concerning Israel are *digested* by part of the Church in the West although, thank God, more and more Christian searchers for truth are not ready to follow this tendency. True believers in Yeshua need to decide which option is more aligned with our faith:

please men in order to avoid conflict or stick to God's will and principles in His word. In order to answer this enigma we first need to know what God's will specifically is concerning probably the main stumbling block in the Middle East conflict: the borders of Israel.

**The borders**

In our desperate attempts to offer a feasible solution for peace in the Middle East, we are often led to propose a change of borders. However, God never intended for His land to be divided and shrunk but on the contrary to extend to wider borders:

*"Your descendants will be like the dust of the earth, and **you will spread out to the west and to the east, to the north and to the south.** All peoples on earth will be blessed through you and your offspring." (Gen.28:14).*

And again:

*"The day for building your walls will come, **the day for extending your boundaries.**" (Mic. 7:11).*

*Extending your boundaries?* This does not sound politically correct today! Yet isn't God able to fulfill His word conveyed by the prophets? Some would be too prompt to cancel the Old Testament verses under the pretense that we are now under a new dispensation, especially regarding the borders of Israel. This is how Old Testament principles can be violated. Nevertheless, they remain valid even under a new dispensation because they are among these irrevocable commandments for all nations:

*"Do not move your neighbor's boundary stone set up by your predecessors in the inheritance you receive in the land the LORD your God is giving you to possess."* (Deut. 19:14).

This commandment is still relevant today concerning the boundaries between the nation of Israel and its surrounding neighbours. Obviously, the world has its way to decide upon borders nowadays. Sometimes it goes according to the last line of military confrontation on the ground and sometimes it is arbitrarily imposed by a coalition of nations or by the United Nations. For instance Texas used to belong to Mexico and no one, not even the state of Mexico would even dare object to the present situation. The point here is not to disagree with what was decided long ago or even question the borders of the greatest nation in the world, but if this is an international principle, it is at least worth pondering why it cannot apply to the borders of Israel that were decided by God long ago and stipulated in His word. It is not even a question of who was first on the land but of whether we agree to submit to God's authority concerning His appointment of tenants and governors of His own land.

Respect for our neighbours' boundaries is a biblical principle generally accepted by believers and unbelievers alike. Israel's borders have definitely been set by her forefathers Abraham, Isaac and Jacob upon God's command and the patriarchs had seen the extent of the borders promised for their descendants. However these boundaries receive even more validity when they are decreed by a higher authority, for it was not the people's decision to conquer land in Moses' or Joshua's time, but rather they were obeying God's command. This is how Jephtah responded to the king of the Ammonites' demand to return the land from the Arnon to the Jabbok:

> *Now since the LORD, the God of Israel, has driven the Amorites out before his people Israel, what right have you to take it over? Will you not take what your god Chemosh gives you?* **Likewise, whatever the LORD our God has given us, we will possess.** *Judges 11:23-25*

Thus the Israelites were animated by a zealous desire to assume the fulfillment of their destiny according to God's own will and admonition. In the days of Moses, God had warned them that their enemies would harass them if His plan of conquest of the land was not implemented on the ground:

> *"But if you do not drive out the inhabitants of the land, those you allow to remain will become barbs in your eyes and thorns in your sides. They will give you trouble in the land where you will live. And then I will do to you what I plan to do to them." (Num. 33:55-56).*

Verse 56 was a severe warning which the sons of Israel did not take as seriously as they should have. They had come to settle on a land flowing with milk and honey and they desired to enjoy peace and prosperity instead of fighting God's war. Many would argue that God, at that time, was cruel and was forcing Israel to interfere into other nations' lives and sovereignty. Yet He knew why He had warned the Israelites against their enemies who would become thorns and briers in their sides. Somebody hampered by thorns in his sides, has a tendency to avoid them and, by doing so, he changes his course. Yet God had given the Israelites both a physical and spiritual journey route and they were supposed to remain faithful to it:

> *So be careful to do what the LORD your God has commanded you;* **do not turn aside to the right or to the left.** *Walk in all the way that the LORD your God has commanded you, so that you may live and prosper and prolong your days in the land that you will possess. Deuteronomy 5:32-33*

It was for this purpose that He had launched the Jewish people into war. One of these reasons, perhaps the main, was to bless the nations not only through the Church but also through Israel from the land, as we will see later on. Hence the Jewish zeal to return to the land has always prevailed in Jewish tradition and culture with a deep sense of being entrusted with a mission toward mankind.

Some understand that the prophecy of the conquest of the land was fulfilled with Joshua. However there are at least two problems with this interpretation:

- First, Joshua didn't conquer the whole land as the Lord spoke to Moses in the plains of Moab:

> *"They did not dislodge the Canaanites living in Gezer; to this day the Canaanites live among the people of Ephraim but are required to do forced labor." (Jos. 16:10).*

It seems that this weakness persisted further on:

*When Israel became strong, they pressed the Canaanites into forced labor **but never drove them out completely**. Nor did Ephraim drive out the Canaanites living in Gezer, but the Canaanites continued to live there among them. Neither did Zebulun drive out the Canaanites living in Kitron or Nahalol, who remained among them; but they did subject them to forced labor. Nor did Asher drive out those living in Acco or Sidon or Ahlab or Aczib or Helbah or Aphek or Rehob, and because of this the people of Asher lived among the Canaanite inhabitants of the land. Neither did Naphtali drive out those living in Beth Shemesh or Beth Anath; but the Naphtalites too lived among the Canaanite inhabitants of the land, and those living in Beth Shemesh and Beth Anath became forced laborers for them. The Amorites confined the Danites to the hill country, not allowing them to come down into the plain. Judges 1:28-35*

This tendency to be slack in the execution of God's command to conquer the whole land had some negative consequences in the course of Israel's history not only for the Jews but also for the Gentiles:

*All the people left from the Amorites, Hittites, Perizzites, Hivites and Jebusites (these peoples were not Israelites), that is, their descendants remaining in the land, whom the Israelites could not exterminate-these*

THE PROMISE OF THE LAND

*Solomon conscripted for his slave labor force, as it is to this day. 1 Kings 9:20-22*

Solomon had to find a way to constrain these people and keep them weak in order to avoid an eventual uprising. This resulted in suffering as these nations remained harshly subdued under the king's leadership.

- Also the command to distribute the land among the Israelites was admonished by God several centuries after Joshua's time through the prophet Ezekiel:

*This is what the Sovereign LORD says: "**These are the boundaries** by which you are to divide the land for an inheritance among the twelve tribes of Israel, with two portions for Joseph. 14 You are to divide it equally among them. Because I swore with uplifted hand to give it to your forefathers, this land will become your inheritance." Ezekiel 47:13-14*

Now we can assume that this prophecy pertains to a messianic era and more specifically to the millennium when Yeshua reigns over the whole earth from Jerusalem. Yet without getting deeply into this topic, it is quite remarkable how this passage remains in line with God's desire to attribute the whole land to the Jewish people as seen in all the scriptures and, although Israel's history had its pauses, the Lord kept His promise of the land intact. As if to make sure that His people would not forget, He reminds the Jews of it through His prophet Ezekiel. Now it is obvious that this prophecy was not fulfilled from Ezekiel's time to the first coming of Yeshua and it is all the more evident as it has not been fully fulfilled in the last 2000 years. So we remain confronted with the decision to believe or not in the veracity of God's word and the only option for true believers remains to pray and wait for the accomplishment of His promise in conformity with His word. This may seem unbearable for some and, to alleviate some present controversies, we do not believe that God wants His people to initiate a conquest of the land today as in Joshua's time. Yeshua remains the Messiah of peace and does not advocate the destruction of other peoples. In fact when God asked the Israelites to exterminate the existing nations living on the land in Joshua's time, it was mainly because of the prevailing abominations and idolatry which desecrated the land. It was also to express His utter repulsion of sin and idolatry. Nonetheless, today He has His ways to fulfill His plan even if it is through Israel's victory in defense over her belligerent enemies.

If we read on in Ezekiel 47 we discover that the boundaries prescribed by the Lord are much beyond the so called *1967 borders* advocated by most nations and, if applied today, they would leave Israel with a territory much bigger than the present one. They would indeed cover most of Syria, the whole of Jordan, part of Iraq, of Saudi Arabia and Egypt, let alone Judea, Samaria including Jerusalem. In fact, even according to the UN resolutions, the 1967 borders were armistice lines supposed to be negotiated, but they were never stipulated as legal final boundaries after the 1967 and 1973 wars.

On the other hand, most of the governments of the world propose a peace process that would include an Israeli withdrawal from the Golan Heights (the biblical Bashan). This unbiblical position is understandable when endorsed by unbelievers, but it would be interesting to hear the position of the Church worldwide in the light of the following passage:

*Shepherd your people with your staff, the flock of your inheritance, which lives by itself in a forest, in fertile pasturelands.* **Let them feed in Bashan and Gilead as in days long ago.** *"As in the days when you came out of Egypt, I will show them my wonders." Nations will see and be ashamed, deprived of all their power. They will lay their hands on their mouths and their ears will become deaf. Micah 7:14-16*

Today in the same way as the Lord expects the Church to adopt a biblical stand on the Golan heights, He also asks the Christians whether His word concerning the Gaza Strip is still relevant:

*Gaza will be abandoned and Ashkelon left in ruins. At midday Ashdod will be emptied and Ekron uprooted. Woe to you who live by the sea, O Kerethite people; the word of the LORD is against you, O Canaan, land of the Philistines. "I will destroy you, and none will be left." The land by the sea, where the Kerethites dwell, will be a place for shepherds and sheep pens.* **It will belong to the remnant of the house of Judah**; *there they will find pasture. In the evening they will lie down in the houses of Ashkelon. The LORD their God will care for them; he will restore their fortunes. Zephaniah 2:4-7*

Before anyone dares to judge God, let us see why verse 7 was declared in prophecy:

*"This they shall have for their pride, because they have reproached and made arrogant threats against the people of the LORD of hosts." (Zeph. 2:10, NKJV).*

Concerning the controversy over Judea and Samaria (or what is commonly called the West Bank), these two regions are certainly within the borders promised to the patriarchs and given to Israel in Ezekiel 47.

Besides, Abraham buried Sarah in Hebron *after* **he bought the ground**. Beth El and Shechem were given to Ephraim's descendants. They were the very places where the patriarchs received God's promises of the land. Therefore it is not surprising that the enemies of Israel, and more precisely the predominantly Muslim Palestinian Authority, have sought to rule these territories, seeking complete dominion over them. The enemy of God's plan is well aware of the symbolism of the battle on the ground and he maneuvers accordingly, but the Lord's 'will for the borders of Israel remains the same yesterday, today and forever. Moreover, there is a biblical principle concerning these borders that many believers and unbelievers alike seem to ignore:

*"When the Most High gave the nations their inheritance, when he divided all mankind, he set up boundaries for the peoples **according to the number of the sons of Israel.**" (Deut. 32:4).*

This is an astounding verse but also a mystery. Of course, like many others of God's principles, this one is again not at all politically correct. The nations would never consider the dependency of their borders on the number of the sons of Israel, unless they are willing to understand and receive God's plan for and through Israel to bless the world. This verse bears witness to the importance that the Lord gives to the sons of Israel and their call regarding the nations, which will be discussed further on.

It is certain that most of the prophecies concerning Israel's future full sovereignty over the land are still awaiting their fulfillment, but it is perplexing that some Christians prefer an international settlement of the conflict with different borders than the ones seen in prophecy. They might be unaware of the implications of this doctrine: it would aim at a foreign occupation of areas of the land that God attributed to the twelve tribes of Israel, knowing that these regions would probably be under Islamic authority. Now it might be useful to remind ourselves here that extreme Islam calls for the death of *the infidels*, Jews and Christians alike, so it would be logical to expect all the Christian leaders and theologians to unite and expose the actual goals of Islamic Fundamentalism but Israel unfortunately remains the focus of criticism. Yet we all know that there are Christians within the Palestinian authority and some of them even in the Gaza strip, but, to our deepest regret, they are far from being in authority and any peace process would have to be attained with the present Muslim Palestinian leaders.

In the prophecy of Ezekiel 47 God makes a clear distinction between the Jews (*the 12 tribes of Israel*) who are to govern the land and the foreigners. This is why the Israeli government has in vain tried to convince the Palestinians to recognize Israel as a Jewish State. However a partial reading of Ezekiel 47 would lead us to conclude that God has no plan for the foreigners in the land, and among them the Arabs, but this is far from the truth. In this chapter, after the Lord calls for a distribution of the land to the twelve tribes of Israel and exposes in details the exact borders of the nation, He declares:

> *"You are to distribute this land among your-selves according to the tribes of Israel. You are to allot it as an inheritance for yourselves and for the aliens who have settled among you and who have children.* **You are to consider them as native-born Israelites; along with you they are to be allotted an inheritance among the tribes of Israel.** *In whatever tribe the alien settles, there you are to give him his inheritance," declares the Sovereign LORD. Ezekiel 47:21-23*

As it is obvious in this passage, God's plan for a peace process is perfect as it calls for a peaceful coex-istence within Israel. Yet, as if to remind us of the con-text of the prophecy, the Lord deemed it necessary to place verse 21 just before dealing with the matter of the foreigners, although its content was already mentioned in verse 13. However nothing leads us to believe that the foreigners will own the land which, as we see at the opening of Ezekiel 47, is distributed to the 12 tribes of Israel. The inheritance of the land for foreigners as seen in Ezekiel 47:22 is different in nature from the distribution of the land to the Jewish people. The first refers to an individual inheritance, the second is the inheritance of a nation and borders are attached to it. The foreigners are allowed to have their plot of ground but Ezekiel 47:21 balances it as a precondition: *"You are to distribute this land among yourselves according to the tribes of Israel"*. So the sovereignty over the enlarged nation with its new borders does not change hands but remains basically Israeli and Jewish. These foreigners will apparently not seek *to throw the Jews into the Sea* (as it has been taught in the Palestinian schools), take over Israel and convert it to Islam as the Islamic Fundamentalists openly declare today, but they will rather accept Jewish authority as they did in David's time. Among them will be some Gentiles who will have contributed to the return of the Jews to their land:

> *"This is what the Sovereign LORD says: 'See, I will beckon to the Gentiles, I will lift up my banner to the peoples; they will bring your sons in their arms and carry your daughters on their shoulders.'" (Is. 49:22).*

In David's time foreigners were attached to the kingdom and were even fighting in the king's army. Uriah the Hittite was a staunch soldier in David's army and Auraunah the Jebusite was ready to give David his plot of land to offer sacrifices to the Lord when the plague was striking Jerusalem. This place was also chosen for the building of Solomon's temple:

> *"Then Solomon began to build the temple of the LORD in Jerusalem on Mount Moriah, where the LORD had appeared to his father David. It was on the threshing floor of **Araunah the Jebusite**, the place provided by David." (2 Chro. 3:1).*

It is therefore not far-fetched for God to implement His plan and bless the foreigners in the land He promised for His people Israel. It is not inconceivable that the Jews and Arabs in Judea and Samaria would live together in peace as it used to be in David's time:

> *The entire assembly of Judah rejoiced, along with the priests and Levites and all who had assembled from Israel, **including the aliens who had come from Israel and those who lived in Judah.** There was great joy in Jerusalem, for since the days of Solomon son of David king of Israel there had been nothing like this in Jerusalem. The priests and the Levites stood to bless the people, and God heard them, for their prayer reached heaven, his holy dwelling place. 2 Chron 30:25-27*

Our unbelief in God's word and our tendency to absorb the trends and fashion of the present age can be a huge obstacle on the way to reconciliation and peace. Foreign kings like king Hiram of Lebanon called Israel *a great nation* (1 Kings 5:7). Israel's mistake so far has been to restrain from investing in Judea and Samaria in the same way the nation has been doing on the Golan Heights. This lack of investments was a clear signal that the Israeli governments never believed that Judea and Samaria were to become an integral part of Israel, according to God's promise. Consequently, the Israeli leaders always behave as though, at some point in the future, these territories would have to be surrendered to *the Palestinians*. This was a grave mistake and the Israeli policy continues in unbelief in this respect instead of holding firm to God's word for today. The Israeli policy so far seems to be inspired by fear and by models inherited from humanism where it should be led by a clear biblical ideology that looks into the future with the courage and faith inspired by a biblical past. In the future God will certainly break the power of Islamic Fundamentalism although the prophecy regarding Ishmael suggested that his descendants would first become indoctrinated by a violent interpretation of Jihad:

> *The angel of the LORD also said to her: "You are now with child and you will have a son. You shall name him Ishmael, for the LORD has heard of your misery. He will be a wild donkey of a man;* ***his hand will be against everyone and everyone's hand against him, and he will live in hostility toward all his brothers.****" Genesis 16:11-12*

In spite of this, we understand through prophecy that the believers in Yeshua will remain faithful to their respective nation and will benefit from God's blessings in Yeshua. Besides, even in the millennium we see the nations still there apparently within their respective boundaries and Israel is no exception, but borders are always controlled and altered by God who alone puts definite final frontiers to each nation according to His incommensurable plan.

The context of Ezekiel 47 presupposes that the foreigners will have accepted Israel's hegemony over the land as God had consistently vowed in the Scriptures. This will be a God-given sentiment to follow His plan for the welfare of all, as it is written: they will be considered as native-born Israelis and will be allotted an inheritance in the land (Ezekiel 47:22). God knew that this promise would not be compatible with the doctrine of those who are calling for Jihad. Besides, the decline and fall of extremist Islam is implied in God's plan in between the lines of Ezekiel 47 because this passage cannot be fulfilled on a territory that would be partly Islamic. After He commanded Joshua to get rid of the Canaanites, today God would not allow foreigners to take authority over the land because, without a drastic change of heart, they would thwart His plan of distribution of the ground to the twelve tribes of Israel. For those who are unaware or naive about the true goal of Israel's enemies, here is what King Farouk of Egypt declared:

> *"The Zionist conquest of Palestine is an affront to all Moslems. There can be no compromise until every Jew is dead and gone."*[7]

Let there be no mistake, this mindset still prevails in some Islamic circles involved in the Middle East conflict today. However God's surpassing wisdom always thwarts the enemy's plan and the schemes of the nations. King Farouk at least said openly what he truly believed. Today some Muslim leaders tend to be more subtle but they would never deny King Farouk's words.

## Chapter 4
# PEACE OR WAR

### Palestinians and Philistines

The Jewish exodus of 70 AD created a territorial vacuum which drew numerous invasions in the course of history. Some of these late occupations like the Turkish and British mandates were very subtle in their ways to deprive the Jewish people of its authority upon the land, but the fact that waves of populations succeeded on the Promised Land did not change God's decision to give it ultimately to His Jewish tenants. Arabs from several parts of the Middle East populated the area and it is only in 1967 that Palestinian terrorist leader Yasser Arafat initiated the notion of a *Palestinian state*. However the truth of the matter is that there has never been a legitimate Palestinian people, let alone a Palestinian nation.

Looking back at historical facts, it was the Roman emperor Hadrian who tried to break the bond between the Jewish people and their homeland by renaming Israel *Palestina*, derived from the word *Philistines*. In 132 AD the Romans defeated the Bar Kochba Jewish revolt and Judea was renamed *Palestina*. Such attempts had one goal: wipe out Jewish claim as a people on their land, but together with this, the intention was also to claim the land for an ancient people who had long ceased to exist: the Philistines. According to the archeologists, they lived on the western coast and principally in the towns of Gaza, Ekron and Ashkelon. Ekron was a center of olive oil production. The Philistines survived until 600 BC at which time nothing much was left of them. Ekron was destroyed in 1000 BC and remained a small insignificant town unable to secure an ongoing existence of the Philistines.

*Philistia* comes from the Hebrew word (paleshet) which means migratory but has in it the root *Palash* meaning *invade*. We know from the Bible that the main cause of war between the Philistines and Israel was an attempt on both sides to gain land, but we also know that names had their importance in God's eyes and for Him the Philistines were the invaders. They had a tendency to oust the Israelites and take over their land, God's land:

> *Isaac planted crops in that land and the same year reaped a hundredfold, because the LORD blessed him. The man became rich, and his wealth continued to grow until he became very wealthy. He had so many flocks and herds and servants that* **the Philistines envied him.** *So all the wells that his father's servants had dug in the time of his father Abraham, the Philistines stopped up, filling them with earth. Genesis 26:12-15*

As we can see, Isaac was the victim of the same offense rooted in deep jealousy. The devil always has the same appealing offers and Israel has been bitterly wounded by his darts:

*"When the Israelites along the valley and those across the Jordan saw that the Israelite army had fled and that Saul and his sons had died, they abandoned their towns and fled. And the Philistines came and occupied them." (1 Sam. 31:7).*

Indeed this rings a bell today and the controversy over Israel is not only the product of ignorance of the history of the land but also the fruit of an intended terminology as Ramon Bennett puts it:

*After the Moslem conquest of Palestina in the 7ᵗʰ century A.D. the name AElia Palestina gradually faded from use. The Arabs called the city Al Quds, and Christians and Jews reverted back to Jerusalem. And in due process time Palestina, the latin form of Philistia – the land of the ancient Philistines – was anglicized into Palestine, the name that is daily placed before our eyes and in our ears by the news media.[8]*

Indeed there are some troubling facts confirming this relation between Palestinian and ancient Philistines.

- First these two terms are identical both in Hebrew and in Arabic and it is not a coincidence that the term *Palestina* was chosen.
- The Romans knew that the Philistines had been enemies of the Jews for many centuries and it is not a secret that the Palestinian leaders are entertaining the same sentiment of enmity. Also, biblically speaking, their desire to deprive the Jews of their land has not disappeared and is at

the center of their vision for an independent nation including present Israel.

- One and a half million Palestinians live in the same region where the Philistines were concentrated and which is called today the *Gaza strip*:

*This is the land that remains: all the regions of the Philistines and Geshurites: from the Shihor River on the east of Egypt to the territory of Ekron on the north, all of it counted as Canaanite (the territory of the five Philistine rulers in Gaza , Ashdod, Ashkelon, Gath and Ekron — that of the Avvites); Joshua 13:2-3*

Today the Palestinians vow to *re-conquer* the whole of *Palestine* and the Jewish cities of Ashdod and Ashkelon have been constantly under rocket attacks from the Gaza strip for at least the last 8 years. With the help of the Hezbollah, Syria, Iran and perhaps even some other Arab countries generally deemed as moderate today, the tactic remains the same and is intelligently expressed in Ramon Bennett's book:

*The political aim of the Arabs is to bypass the biblical Israelites and claim kinship with the Canaanites, the pre-Israelite inhabitants of the land. Then it becomes possible to assert an historical claim antedating the biblical promise and the subsequent possession of the land by the Jews. The Moslems intend to disconnect the Jewish people from their history in their homeland and have them appear as recent interlopers, thus providing the rationale for their removal or annihilation.[9]*

Although we do not agree with the general inclusion of *Arabs* and *Moslems*, this has certainly been the Palestinian policy and the stand of several Arab Muslim leaders. The Palestinians have not only been led by the same rationale but they have succeeded in propagating it to the whole world by their persisting presence and a clever brainwashing of the world media.

## A conflict of spiritual nature

The Middle East conflict is generally approached from a pure political standpoint and, although the developments in this region have political implications, it would be misleading to ignore the spiritual background. In this respect it is helpful to go to the source in God's word and try to understand the roots and the consequences of the dispute. By studying the biblical history of the Philistines and their relations with Israel, much can be learned about the Palestinian belligerency against the Jewish State, but we must remember that God uses the enemies of Israel to discipline His people and there is no doubt that the Philistines were used by God as a rod of correction:

> *And Samuel said to the whole house of Israel, "If you are returning to the LORD with all your hearts, then rid yourselves of the foreign gods and the Ashtoreths and commit yourselves to the LORD and serve him only, and* **he will deliver you out of the hand of the Philistines.**" *1 Samuel 7:3*

Nevertheless this does in no way elude God's sentiment about the cities of the Philistines: they were to belong to Israel:

*So the Philistines were subdued and did not invade Israelite territory again. Throughout Samuel's lifetime, the hand of the LORD was against the Philistines. The towns from Ekron to Gath that the Philistines had captured from Israel were **restored to her**, and Israel delivered the neighboring territory from the power of the Philistines. And there was peace between Israel and the Amorites.*
*1 Samuel 7:13-14*

The Bible makes it clear that the towns from Ekron to Gath used to belong to the Philistines, but that the Lord had destined them to the Israelites and that they had to be restored to them soon or later. Nevertheless the Philistines were indeed thorns and briers in the Israelites' eyes for many centuries. We see them in Genesis 21 and they remain Israel's enemies under King Hezekiah. Yet God's decree about their destiny remained valid and they were vowed to complete destruction (Zephaniah 2:4-7) but there are some pertinent verses which shed light on the reasons why the Lord was so determined to do away with this foreign people:

*"This is what the Sovereign LORD says: 'Because the Philistines acted in vengeance and took revenge with **malice in their hearts**, and with **ancient hostility** sought to destroy Judah,'" (Ezek. 25:15).*

This malice was utterly displeasing to God and today it is not a coincidence that the Palestinian leaders and other terrorist groups vent the same sentiment. It has unfortunately filtered down to a majority of indoctrinated people in the Gaza Strip and unfortunately also in the Palestinian Authority. For many years the education system and curriculum in the Palestinian schools have been impregnated with a visceral hatred of the Jew who has been constantly caricatured as the modern Nazi. Ezekiel 25:15 goes further to evoke an *ancient hostility*. In fact the Hebrew term for ancient is *olam* meaning also *eternal* or often used in the expression *forever*. This leads us to understand that this hostility was not just a temporary sentiment but an ancient spirit of enmity attacking God's people at all times, especially when we see today the same root name appearing again, embodied by Palestinians with the same aggressive spirit. Nevertheless there are those in the Palestinian authority who are craving for peace as much as the Israelis, but they tend to be intimidated and scared by a rising aversion toward the Jews amidst their own people. It is sad that many of them left the Palestinian cities like Bethlehem for instance and immigrated to the U.S.A. or Canada. Yet those remaining may well be a factor of hope if they grasp the revelation of the riches to be obtained by their unity with Israel.

Of course the Philistines disappeared long ago and it would be ridiculous to suggest an ethnical descent with the Palestinians yet he same spirit remains unfortunately an actuality. It is at least puzzling why the Palestinians saw fit to adopt this name, knowing fair well what the Philistines used to represent in God's eyes as well as the future He prophesied for them. Moreover, the war between the Philistines and God's people was not just physical but involved their god and the God of Israel:

*After the Philistines had captured the ark of God, they took it from Ebenezer to Ashdod.*

111

*Then they carried the ark into Dagon's temple and set it beside Dagon . When the people of Ashdod rose early the next day, there was Dagon , fallen on his face on the ground before the ark of the LORD! They took Dagon and put him back in his place. But the following morning when they rose, there was **Dagon , fallen on his face on the ground before the ark of the LORD!** His head and hands had been broken off and were lying on the threshold; only his body remained. 1 Samuel 5:1-4*

The Lord wanted to make very clear to the Philistines and perhaps also to the Israelites that He was the supreme God and that nobody else would receive the glory before Him. In this passage of scriptures, the Philistines became aware that their god could not defeat the God of Israel, although they used to believe in and evoke Dagon in times of war in the past:

*Now the rulers of the Philistines assembled to offer a great sacrifice to Dagon their god and to celebrate, saying, "Our god has delivered Samson, our enemy, into our hands." When the people saw him, they praised their god, saying, "Our god has delivered our enemy into our hands, the one who laid waste our land and multiplied our slain." Judges 16:23-24*

God sent plagues to the Philistines (1 Samuel 5:6) and even their priests became aware that they had to deal with a situation which was spiritual in nature. They consequently reprimanded their own people with the following words:

*"Why do you harden your hearts as the Egyptians and Pharaoh did? When he treated them harshly, did they not send the Israelites out so they could go on their way?" (1 Sam. 6:6).*

Whether we like it or not we find the same parallel nowadays: on the one hand we see the nation of Israel on its land, revering the God of Abraham, Isaac and Jacob, and on the other hand some Arab nations, the Palestinians among them, subjugated by Allah, the God of Islam and fiercely opposed to Israel as a nation. The Philistines opposed any turn of situation initiated by the God of Israel. For instance, see how defiant they became when the Lord intended to promote David as king:

*When the Philistines heard that David had been anointed king over Israel, **they went up in full force to search for him**, but David heard about it and went down to the stronghold. Now the Philistines had come and spread out in the Valley of Rephaim; so David inquired of the LORD, "Shall I go and attack the Philistines? Will you hand them over to me?" The LORD answered him, "Go, for I will surely hand the Philistines over to you." 2 Samuel 5:17-19*

The same David was destined to be in the descendant lineage of the Messiah Yeshua Son of David. David who was also supposed to be king over Israel with enlarged borders and this is why the spirit of the Philistines was so enraged. In fact, beyond pursuing the Israelites in their wars they were confronting the God of Israel.

In the Bible we see how, in their obdurate struggle against Israel, the Philistines were very prompt to join in coalition with another ethnic people:

> *The LORD aroused against Jehoram **the hostility of the Philistines and of the Arabs** who lived near the Cushites. They **attacked** Judah, invaded it and **carried off** all the goods found in the king's palace, together with his sons and wives. Not a son was left to him except Ahaziah the youngest. 2 Chronicles 21:16-17*

It is very striking to see these two together in hostility against Israel: the Philistines and the Arabs, but this is not a mere coincidence for it keeps recurring. For instance, when the Lord decides to reset the balance of forces between Israel and her belligerents, we find these two enemies coupled again

> *The fear of the LORD fell on all the kingdoms of the lands surrounding Judah, so that they did not make war with Jehoshaphat." Some **Philistines** brought Jehoshaphat gifts and silver as tribute**, and the Arabs** brought him flocks: seven thousand seven hundred rams and seven thousand seven hundred goats. 2 Chronicles 17:10-11*

We see the same hostile spirit in play especially when the Jews intend to settle on the land and rebuild Jerusalem after the Babylonian exile:

*But when Sanballat, Tobiah, **the Arabs,** the Ammonites and **the men of Ashdod** heard that the repairs to Jerusalem's walls had gone ahead and that the gaps were being closed, they were **very angry.** They all **plotted** together to come and fight against Jerusalem and **stir up trouble** against it. **But we prayed** to our God and posted a guard day and night to meet this threat. Nehemiah 4:7-9*

In the present time, we witness the same obduracy to refuse the Jews their God-given sovereignty over Jerusalem. In their wars against the Jews, many of the extremist Muslim Arabs strangely manifest the same cruel spirit of terrorism as we saw in the days of old:

*"The people of Jerusalem made Ahaziah, **Jehoram's youngest son,** king in his place, **since the raiders, who came with the Arabs into the camp, had killed all the older sons.** So Ahaziah son of Jehoram king of Judah began to reign." (2 Chr. 22:1).*

Today the target remains adamantly the same: the civilian Jews. One needs to be really ill-informed to ignore the Palestinian rockets, the bomb blasts in Israeli buses, the incursions into Jewish homes and liquidations of whole families, including infants, as in the terrorist attack on the Vogel family butchered in the Jewish settlement of Itamar on March 11th, 2011.

Anyone with a minimum of spiritual discernment would recognize the devilish spirits behind such acts of horror. This is just another evidence bearing witness to the sort of war we are in, as Ken Burnett wrote:

*If we are to understand the will of the Lord, we will see the Middle East not just as some huge political crisis, but as a battle of light against darkness, of right against wrong – the greatest such battle since Satan unleashed his fury against Israel's Messiah and now against Messiah's own people and land*[10]

However, while God uses enemies to discipline Israel, He abhors their malicious and cruel heart when they rejoice and distribute sweets in the streets of Ramalah or Gaza following the bombing of a bus by terrorists in Tel Aviv, killing adults and children alike. Although it is true that there is a human Palestinian problem that we will go into later on, it is the heart that God examines as He has always done, without exception of race or culture:

*For this is what the Sovereign LORD says: Because you have clapped your hands and stamped your feet, **rejoicing with all the malice of your heart against the land of Israel,** therefore I will stretch out my hand against you and give you as plunder to the nations. I will cut you off from the nations and exterminate you from the countries. I will destroy you, and you will know that I am the LORD. Ezekiel 25:6-7*

It would be wise for *fulfillment theology* preachers to present these passages of scriptures and caution their listeners as the Lord does in these verses, or can we presume that God is not the same yesterday, today and forever? As preachers we have a high calling toward our audience and we will be first to be held responsible before God if we conceal His truth and warnings.

Beyond the constant historical opposition and attacks on the Jewish people, it is remarkable to notice the spirit at work. In ancient times Amalek would not only attack civilians, he would also choose the weak and the defenseless, the Israelites who were dropping behind in the desert because they were slower than their brothers (Deuteronomy 25:17-18). Yet the Lord's response was determined and without appeal:

*"When the LORD your God gives you rest from all the enemies around you in the land he is giving you to possess as an inheritance, you shall blot out the memory of Amalek from under heaven. Do not forget!" (Deut. 25:19).*

Indeed the ancient spirit of the Arabs and the Philistines as suggested in the scriptures is not dead and it is still active when Israel's enemies consider terrorism, often striking blindly within the Israeli population, as a legitimate option. Here we have to make a crucial difference between the spiritual and the physical, for not all the Arabs are animated by the same cruelty, but it is crucial to identify the spirit in action. Our struggle is not against flesh and blood although this tends to often be forgotten when spiritual warfare is materialized by wars between nations.

It is striking that some Arab factions surrounding Israel, albeit disunited and even fighting each other as it is the case in Syria, have one common sentiment: the hatred of the Jew. The Hezbollah, the Hamas, the PLO, the Jihad, El Qaida and more, all have one common goal: to oust the Jewish nation from the Middle East. The same spirit is at work in them and particularly in those who have been indoctrinated to violence by interpretations of teachings of the Koran as we will show in the next chapter.

Presenting the Middle East conflict as a religious war is not the whole truth as it supposes that the two sides are wrong and God is not involved. This is the tactic that the devil has always used to discredit religion and it is also the excuse that the nations bring forth to offer a humanistic solution, excluding God from the scene. The truth of the matter is that God is defending His land, His people and His Church under His own rules despite the whim and caprice of the nations who, at some point, will have to choose to fight Him or trust Him. This is what gives the conflict a spiritual nature that cannot be ignored, as Paul Wilkinson said:

> *Goliath cannot be felled with a stone and a sling as in the days of King David, because the problem isn't political, the problem isn't sociological, the problem isn't about lack of education or lack of dialogue, the problem is a spiritual one. The problem is that there is an adversary of God, of Israel, of Christians.* [11]

As we contemplate the developments of the situation in the Middle East, it is undeniable that God is in control of all the events evolving on the ground. He keeps a balance of forces according to His plan and His will, not giving complete victory to any side until His appointed time, but many lives would be spared if men had a minimum knowledge of His word and His ways. This is why this ongoing confrontation on the ground must be approached from a biblical standpoint.

## A peace process or a trap

First let's ponder a little on some roots of anti-Semitism in some Arab and Islamic circles. Although the word *Jihad* is well known in the whole world, many people choose to ignore what really lies behind it. Here are just a couple of Quran excerpts which, when interpreted by the letter, can have devastating consequences:

> *"O you who believe! do not take the Jews and the Christians for friends; they are friends of each other; and whoever amongst you takes them for a friend, then surely he is one of them; surely Allah does not guide the unjust people."[12]*

Please notice that the Christians are put in the same bag as the Jews! May whoever has ears hear! This raises a question: would there be an ancient spirit at work today? If this is the case we need to know how to address it in prayer and worship but in the same time to love the Arabs and the Muslims. Here is one other intriguing passage of the Koran which has been interpreted as a call to anti-Semitism:

> *"Fight those who do not believe in Allah...nor follow the religion of truth, out of those who have been given the Book, until they pay the tax in acknowledgment of superiority and they are in a state of subjection."[13]*

119

Of course there are different practical implications and interpretations of the Koran but Islamist extremists tend to depart from the moderate religion that Islam was a few decades ago. Please take note of what *Al Qibla*, the daily newspaper of Mecca printed on March 23, 1918 in support of the Balfour Declaration of 1917:

> *The resources of the country [Palestine] are still virgin soil and will be developed by the Jewish immigrants (...) we have seen the Jews from foreign countries streaming to Palestine from Russia, Germany, Austria, Spain, and America. The cause of causes could not escape those who had a gift of deeper insight. They knew that the country was for its original sons [abna'ihi-l-asliyin], for all their differences, a sacred and beloved homeland. The return of these exiles [jaliya] to their homeland will prove materially and spiritually an experimental school for their brethren who are with them in the fields, factories, trades and all things connected to the land.[14]*

We would dream to read such comments in any Arab newspaper nowadays but, alas, much of the world media have been deceived by the modern Islamic fundamentalist propaganda. In the West, one generally tends to believe that the God of Islam is, after all, the same as the God of Abraham, Isaac and Jacob. However this is a serious mistake. The God of Islam excludes Isaac as the son of Abraham brought as a sacrifice to the Lord. Islam believes it was Ishmael, but the New Testament tells us that the Messiah Yeshua is a descendant of Isaac and Jacob, not of Ishmael.

For Islam *God has no son*, therefore the genealogy of the Messiah is entirely truncated in the Islamic mentality. This is why Jesus is often depicted as a Palestinian but with no reference to His Jewish origin or to His Messianic identity. This thinking has serious implications on the Muslim and Palestinian mindset today when considering a peace process in the Middle East. It is not accidental that Israel has a real hard time believing the Arab Muslim nations or Islamic organizations concerning an eventual peace process:

> *"I am a man of peace; but when I speak, they are for war." (Ps. 120:7).*

As a result of all the above, the 2000 years old quest for peace finds but flimsy faith among the Israelis today. Historical facts are just too convincing and tend to make the Israelis hopeless of living in peace with their neighbours. A long history of events, declarations and disappointments left the Israelis with the sense that there is no partner for peace on the other side. On the other hand, as believers, we should keep aware of the Lord's warnings concerning any treaty which would sell land for peace. We do have a God of peace but not peace at any price. The Lord will never suffer to see His goals thwarted for a man-made ideal of a lower standard.

God regarded King Joshaphat as a good king. He was not a warmonger and it was with good intention that he sought a peace treaty with King Ahab (2 Chronicles 18), but it didn't take long till God gave him His own view on the king's well intended policy:

> *When Jehoshaphat king of Judah returned safely to his palace in Jerusalem, Jehu the*

*seer, the son of Hanani, went out to meet him and said to the king, **"Should you help the wicked and love those who hate the LORD?** Because of this, the wrath of the LORD is upon you."* 2 Chronicles 19:1-2

Here again we can see how God used a war to expose the true heart condition of the leaders involved. The Lord expected the king to oppose those whom God opposed. This matter of making a treaty with enemies without the Lord's approval recurred several times in the history of the Jewish people. King Ahab made a treaty with Ben Hadad even after the Lord gave him (Ahab) the victory. However this was a grave mistake and God's sentence was quick to come:

*"He said to the king, 'This is what the LORD says: "You have set free a man I had determined should die. Therefore it is your life for his life, your people for his people."'* (1 Kings 20:42).

Today, for us who live according to the new Covenant, the battle is not against flesh and blood but it is certainly against the spirits at work. The Lord does not hate people but He does abhor their ways whenever they are not aligned with His. He also knows men's schemes and seeks to protect those who are His own. This is why He cautioned the Israelites very early in their walk with Him:

*"Be careful not to make a treaty with those who live in the land where you are going, or they will be **a snare** among you."* (Ex. 34:12).

122

The Hebrew term for *snare* is *mokesh*. Actually, in today's context of the Middle East conflict, it is interesting to mark that, in modern Hebrew, the same word is used to describe a mine. The connotation is of something which suddenly explodes under your feet and this is an accurate picture of the danger on the ground in Israel. Beyond all the international laws and guaranties, a peace treaty requires a minimum of trust. Unfortunately, several past events and episodes have eroded this trust and, without getting into numerous minute details, we can enumerate some of them.

Starting from the North, in 1982 in response to the terrorist attacks coming through the northern border, Israel decided to occupy South Lebanon and help the Christian Maronite militias against the Hezbollah. In year 2000 the Israeli government led by Prime Minister Ehud Barak decided to unilaterally withdraw the Israeli forces from South Lebanon as was the demand of the Hezbollah and the puppet Lebanese government controlled by Syria. However, this unilateral gesture of good will did not stop the Hezbollah's attacks and it was followed by the kidnap of three Israeli soldiers. In 2006 Hezbollah started to shell Israeli villages across the borders, which triggered an Israeli incursion into Lebanon. In the ceasefire, one of the UN conditions was that Hezbollah would retreat north of the Litany River. Well, soon after that the Hezbollah was back right across the Israeli–Lebanese border, with tens of thousands of missiles ready to be fired on civilian habitations in the Galilee and Tel Aviv, and all this in complete violation of the UN implemented ceasefire agreement.

In the South, Israel withdrew from the Gaza Strip again as a peace building sign of good will. It was part of an Israeli peace initiative called *Gaza first*. It was an excellent opportunity for the Palestinians to engage into onward peace talks with the Israeli government. In August 2005 the I.D.F. engaged in a heart breaking evacuation of the Jewish settlers who saw themselves uprooted by their own army brothers from the land of their forefathers, leaving behind them a blooming agriculture as well as newly built houses and synagogues. These were soon destroyed by the Hamas to be replaced by rocket and missile launchers. As a militant of the Hamas explained to a reporter of the French newspaper Le Monde (16/12/2012):

*"We follow Abas so that he may obtain a Palestinian state on the basis of the 1967 borders; once this goal is reached, the Hamas will pursue its goal, the liberation of the whole Palestine, from the river [the Jordan river] to the Sea [the Mediterranean]."*

At a meeting in Gaza celebrating the 25th anniversary of the Hamas organization, Khaled Mashal declared that he would not concede one inch of *Palestine*, meaning the whole of Israel. For the Israeli government, such inflammatory declarations, among other acts of hostility are enough to justify the Israeli blockade in the Mediterranean Sea. It has but one goal: prevent any arm smuggling from the sea into the Gaza Strip, at least until the Gaza leaders are ready to consider peace with Israel as a plausible option. The Palestinians have the same old goal that all the enemies of Israel have always had: the destruction of God's people and the occupation of His land:

*O God, do not keep silent; be not quiet, O God, be not still. See how your enemies are astir, how your foes rear their heads. With* *cunning they conspire against your people; they plot against those you cherish. **"Come," they say, "let us destroy them as a nation, that the name of Israel be remembered no more."** (Psalms 83:1-4)*

In the East the PLO seeks the recognition of Palestine as a nation but on the other hand refuses to recognize Israel as a Jewish State, knowing it would give the Jewish people biblical legitimacy rooted in God's word. In February 2012 Mahmud Abbas, the leader of the Palestinian authority declared in his victory speech:

*"One day, a young Palestinian will raise the Palestinian flag over Jerusalem", he vowed, "the eternal capital of the state of Palestine".[15]*

It is noteworthy that the Palestinians have always spoken of Jerusalem, and not East Jerusalem, as the capital of the eventual *state of Palestine*, knowing that this view is in direct confrontation with what both Jews and Christians uphold as God's word. Yet the Arab leaders do not leave any ground for doubt by reaffirming that Arab, and more specifically Moslem sovereignty over Jerusalem is but a matter of time. In March 2013, the emir of Qatar, Sheikh Hamad bin Khalifa al-Thani proposed creating a $1 billion fund for the defense of Jerusalem's Arab identity. He said Qatar would contribute $250 million to the fund, adding that he expected other Arab nations to come up with the rest:

*"The Palestinian, Arab and Muslim rights in Jerusalem are not negotiable and Israel must realize this,"* the emir said.[16]

Besides, the insistence of the nations to divide the city of the Great King is in direct opposition with a clear biblical principle:

> *Jerusalem is built like a city that is **closely compacted together**. That is where the tribes go up, the tribes of the LORD, to praise the name of the LORD according to the statute given to Israel. There the thrones for judgment stand, the thrones of the house of David. Psalms 122:3-5*

The expression *closely compacted together* in Hebrew gives the clear idea of complete unity and an indivisible entity. It points to God's goal concerning this city. It is the capital of the twelve tribes of Israel. While it is true that even the Jews will worship Him in spirit and in truth, they will go up to Jerusalem to worship corporately with the nations at some specific symbolical festival dates. The *two states* solution, as advocated by the Palestinians and most of the nations, would call for a division of Jerusalem, bearing social and spiritual ramifications: it would deepen the already existing gap between Jews and Arabs but it would also present a huge problem for the city both from a functional, religious and social standpoint. For instance, there are religious sites connected with two or three religions and a division would cause enormous tensions. Just a small reminder: The religious sites started to be accessible to the three religions only after the Israeli army took possession of the city in 1967. Before that, the Arabs never allowed free access to these sites, certainly not to the Jews. It is ironic that the same people who are so vociferously opposed to the building of the wall between Israel and the so-called West Bank are so in favour of a fence or another wall within Jerusalem, where both Arabs and Jews are learning to live and work together. Spiritually we need to keep in mind that Jerusalem also suggests the spiritual abode of the Body of Messiah, a city on the hill:

> *'Consequently, you are no longer foreigners and aliens, but fellow citizens with God's people and members of God's household, built on the foundation of the apostles and prophets, with Christ Jesus himself as the chief cornerstone." (Eph. 2:19-20).*

The division of the city infers, in a subtle way, the division of God's kingdom, the New Jerusalem, as the present Jerusalem is its earthly counterpart, and this is precisely what the enemy is suggesting as he knows and opposes some biblical principles:

> *"Jesus knew their thoughts and said to them, 'Every kingdom divided against itself will be ruined, and every city or household divided against itself will not stand.'" (Matt. 12:25).*

It is obvious that the city of Jerusalem seen in prophecy in the Millennium will not be divided between Jews and Muslims and a decision to divide it today would not be in keeping with God's word:

> *"For David had said, 'Since the LORD, **the God of Israel**, has granted rest to **his people** and has come to dwell in Jerusalem forever'" (1 Chr. 23:25).*

127

It is remarkable how the peace proposals of the modern Philistines contradict any biblical principle concerning the land. Moreover in May 2011 a pact was signed between Abbas and the Hamas to eradicate any misunderstanding which would lead to think that the Palestinian Authority has nothing to do with that terrorist organization in the Gaza Strip. It isn't surprising that this engagement was considered by Netanyahu as *"a mortal blow to peace and a great victory for terrorism"[17]*.

In the light of the above, what kind of peace could Israel expect? The only option left to the Jews would be to deny God's biblical promises. Because of the pressures on the ground, the Jewish State has a recurring tendency to relinquish portions of the land in return for an illusory peace, but God's original plan for Israel to settle on these territories remains unflinching, although it does not sound politically correct today. Sadly, despite Israel's almost naïve belief, peace never became a reality and the Jewish nation still tends to act according to the same old pattern as seen in biblical times:

> *"And be sure to say, 'Your servant Jacob is coming behind us.' **For he thought, 'I will pacify him with these gifts I am sending on ahead**; later, when I see him, perhaps he will receive me.'" (Gen. 32:20).*

This tactic may sometimes work for a season, as it was the case between Jacob and Esau, but did Jacob trust Esau? Not really. He sought to *pacify him with gifts*. Doesn't it apply to the present conflict? Israel has repeatedly tried to pacify her enemies with territorial and political concessions. Did the Jews get any peace in return? Not quite, to put it mildly. Did Esau strike a genuine lasting peace agreement with his brother

Jacob? A study of the descendants of Esau and their ongoing hostility against the Jewish people shows that the answer to this question is rather negative. Unfortunately the same roots bear the same fruits. Esau went to settle in Seir but, in obedience to his Lord, Jacob went to Succoth, an ancient town located in what is commonly called Transjordan. Esau's attempt to pull Jacob to Seir was in fact, both an act of rebellion against the Lord and a complete misunderstanding of His long-term plans. The purpose of Israel's enemies has always been to draw the Jews away from their land:

> *Do not listen to Hezekiah. This is what the king of Assyria says: Make peace with me and come out to me. Then every one of you will eat from his own vine and fig tree and drink water from his own cistern, **until I come and take you to a land like your own**, a land of grain and new wine, a land of bread and vineyards, a land of olive trees and honey. Choose life and not death! 2 Kings 18:31-32*

Notice the bait in verse 32, how the enemy tries to imitate God by offering His people a fake land? This is still what the he lays before Israel's eyes to seduce her into other illusory paths.

Some believers may think that it is too early for God to implement His plan on the ground and that, in the meantime, Israel needs to settle with some kind of compromise. However, we need to bear in mind that any compromise would de facto lead to a definitive division of the land and its exchange for some flimsy peace. Even if this option were to be taken seriously, its consequences would militarily put Israel in a precarious position as we will see further on.

In April 1920 the San Remo resolution stipulated the right for the Jewish people to their own land and even the Jewish settlements in Judea and Samaria are covered in article 6 of the Mandate of Palestine. It clearly mentions that *"the world has the obligation to help the Jews settle there"*.[18]

In this resolution, the Balfour Declaration called for a national home for the Jewish people. These documents are actually the last juridical mandates that Israel could use in international court. This international law has never been abrogated, therefore the Jewish settlements in what is commonly called the West Bank are legal. They actually fit quite perfectly with God's plan seen in Ezekiel 47, but today the international efforts aim at violating the San Remo Resolution, uproot the Jewish settlements and declare a Palestinian state, which, by the way, doesn't figure anywhere in biblical prophecy. In the past some nations tried their utmost to deprive Israel of any way of defense against her enemies. On the 30th of December 1942, at the same time when myriads of Jews were sent to the concentration camps, Ben Gurion gave a speech which couldn't be made wholly public because some passages were censured by the British government. Here is the main censured part of the speech:

*In the name of all the Jews, we demand from you, leaders of Great Britain, Russia and America, our right of a Jewish army. Our right to fight against the worst of our enemies as Jews, in a Jewish framework, in a Jewish organization, with a Jewish leadership, under Jewish discipline and a Jewish flag.*

*We will not be satisfied with crumbs which*
*have been given to us for the defense of our*
*homeland and of the surrounding countries.*
*Not only as sons of Israel but as Jews and*
*for being Jewish.*[19]

This British policy purposed to keep Palestine as such and to thwart Jewish sovereignty on the land. Today all the world media are orchestrating a huge campaign to promote a Palestinian state next to Israel. However this new state, with the most likely participation of the Hamas, would present a tangible danger for Israel inasmuch as it would bring the Jewish nation back to the 1967 borders and would leave roughly 10 miles from the Mediterranean Sea to Transjordan. It would de facto create a Palestinian enclave into Israeli territory and make the Jewish State very vulnerable in case of conflict. It would take between two to four minutes for any hostile aircraft to attack Israel. In order to intercept such an attack the Israeli defense would need to counterattack 10 miles beyond the border...practically mission impossible. In fact, according to UN resolution 242 Israel is not called to withdraw from the West Bank and the resolution did not include any talks about land swaps, neither did it define the extent of an eventual Israeli withdrawal. It just called on the parties to strike an agreement until a just and lasting peace in the Middle East is achieved.

The return of the Palestinian refugees, so adamantly demanded in any peace talks, is obviously unacceptable for the Jewish State. Nevertheless the refugee problem has formed a methodology in the Arab world. After 1948, 600,000 Arabs refused to stay under Israeli nationality because they were promised by the Muslims to be able to return to their land and houses after an expected Arab victory over the Jews.

They became refugees in Lebanon but were refused the same rights as the Lebanese. One of the conditions of the Palestinian Authority for any peace settlement is the return of 1.4 million refugees to Israeli territory, knowing quite well that many of them would be terrorists coming back to Israel with the only goal to start an uprising and *re-conquer Palestine.*

Another argument used by the pro-Palestinians relates to the building of the wall separating Jewish settlements from Palestinian villages. However, their opposition to this wall is not motivated by a genuine desire to have Jews and Arabs united in peace but rather to leave free access to Palestinian suicide bombers into Israel. According to statistics published by the Israeli government, between 2000 and July 2003, when the first continuous segment of the barrier was built, 73 Palestinian suicide bombings were carried out from the West Bank, killing 293 Israelis and injuring over 1,900. However, from August 2003 to the end of 2006, only 12 attacks were carried out, killing 64 Israelis and wounding 445).[20]

In 2012 the terrorist attacks were reduced much below these figures and are now becoming practically non-existent. Nobody likes walls but when fences and walls are protective and are actually saving lives, they become a must until the dust settles and common sense returns to the region.

Consequently, the chances for a man-made peace process look very thin and the present situation can be very frustrating. Despair can sink in our hearts unless we remember God's plan and stick to His word. It is not a coincidence that the Lord blocked all the gates to a pseudo peace that would fail to be aligned with His sovereign word, until the Church and the nations realize the cost and responsibility of their position toward Israel at such a time as this. Of course God is faithful to implement His word through His Son and the Church should be first to recognize it:

*"he says: 'It is too small a thing for you to be my servant to restore the tribes of Jacob and bring back those of Israel I have kept. I will also make you a light for the Gentiles, that you may bring my salvation to the ends of the earth.'" (Is. 49:6).*

Meanwhile the Jews are learning God's lesson, often falling short of His will and of their mission. Israel may be a holy land but certainly not a holy people. Looking at the facts makes us realize that the Jewish State has done a lot to pacify its enemies. According to the World Health Organization's February 2012 report, 91.5% of the Palestinian requests for medical treatment in the Israeli hospitals were approved and carried out, and 7.2% are currently under review. The Israeli government treats these cases with importance and urgency, as reflected by the statistics. As the civil war is raging in Syria, the wounded are regularly brought to the fence to be transported to Israeli hospitals where they can be sure of fair treatment. The Israeli authorities declared several times that they would not discriminate between them but would fully cover the hospital costs until these people recover and can be released. For decades the Israeli government has pushed funds and humanitarian aid into Palestinian territory, including the Gaza Strip where the rocket launchers are set up, without seeing any sign of good will in return. Instead, in order to gore Israel, on the 29th of November 2012, the nations abstained or voted on behalf of a representation of *Palestine* as a non-voting member at the UN assembly. This was intended to be the first unilateral step toward the recognition of Palestine's full membership in the UN.

However, in the present situation it is obvious that both Israelis and Palestinians have their share of suffering, but God is still in control with a message of and a way to peace still rejected by the nations. In his book "the land of many names" Steve Maltz wrote:

> A grave danger is to be sidetracked by human issues. Yes, the Palestinians have had a hard deal, though not just at the hand of the Israelis. Yes, they have suffered to an extent under Israeli rule, just as they suffered in Jordan and Lebanon. Prejudices are a fact of fallen humanity. Ask a black man in the USA or an Aborigene in Australia. These are issues of human rights and inequality. But all these concerns pale into insignificance when divine issues come into plane[21]

It is therefore important in the present situation, for the Jewish State to learn from past mistakes and know how to act in righteousness toward the Gentiles on the ground. This is a process but in the last 10 years, Israel has indeed learnt lessons from past mistakes. Yet God's plan must not be altered until the Palestinians trust the Lord and true biblical unity with Israel is installed in the Middle East:

> In that day there will be a highway from Egypt to Assyria. The Assyrians will go to Egypt and the Egyptians to Assyria. The Egyptians and Assyrians will worship together. In that day Israel will be the third, along with Egypt and

*Assyria, a blessing on the earth. The LORD Almighty will bless them, saying, "Blessed be Egypt my people, Assyria my handiwork, and Israel my inheritance." Isaiah 19:23-25*

Unfortunately the preceding verses of this chapter show that the way to the fulfillment of this prophecy is not without God's pressure upon the Gentiles involved, at least Egypt. Meanwhile Israel's enemies keep falling into the same traps, separating themselves further from God. Surely the Lord is in control and the attacks from Israel's enemies are used by God to correct His people, but they are also used to demonstrate His might and to reveal His final victory:

*Therefore, son of man, prophesy and say to Gog: "This is what the Sovereign LORD says: In that day, when my people Israel are living in safety, will you not take notice of it? You will come from your place in the far north, you and many nations with you, all of them riding on horses, a great horde, a mighty army. You will advance against my people Israel like a cloud that covers the land. In days to come, O Gog, **I will bring you against my land, so that the nations may know me when I show myself holy through you before their eyes.**" Ezekiel 38:14-16*

The Lord Himself will bring the nations against His land so that they may know Him, but let there be no mistake about the aftermath of the battle:

*I will summon a sword against Gog on all my mountains, declares the Sovereign*

135

*LORD. Every man's sword will be against his brother. I will execute judgment upon him with plague and bloodshed; I will pour down torrents of rain, hailstones and burning sulfur on him and on his troops and on the many nations with him. And so I will show my greatness and my holiness, and I will make myself known in the sight of many nations. Then they will know that I am the LORD. Ezekiel 38:21-23*

The enemies of Israel, in their ignorance of God's word, are heading into a wall and this wall is God Himself. While Israel suffers loss, a remnant will be preserved for the Lord to unfold His plan through His people:

*"'Surely the eyes of the Sovereign LORD are on the sinful kingdom. I will destroy it from the face of the earth — yet I will not totally destroy the house of Jacob,' declares the LORD." (Amos. 9:8).*

It is essential to understand that, although God's judgment toward Israel is severe, His plan for the Jewish overcomers is all the more rewarding:

*"In that day the remnant of Israel, **the survivors of the house of Jacob**, will no longer rely on him who struck them down but will truly rely on the LORD, the Holy One of Israel. A remnant will return, **a remnant of Jacob will return to the Mighty God**." (Is. 10:20-21).*

## Chapter 5

# GOD'S PLAN FOR AND THROUGH ISRAEL ON HER LAND

### Jacob and Israel

I n order to deeply understand the prophecies concerning the restoration and call of Israel in the end
times, which we will examine in a further chapter, we
need to grasp the significance of Jacob's change of
name. In the episode related in Genesis 32, Jacob
was cornered in a desperate situation. He knew that
his brother Esau was not coming with 400 men just to
greet him. His brother had nourished deep resentment
in his heart and he was determined not to miss this
opportunity to get his revenge. Jacob acted swiftly and
wisely to pacify his brother and protect his family. In a
desperate attempt to secure his posterity, he divided
his people into two groups and sent them separately.
Then he prayed and sent gifts ahead to his brother
to assuage him. At the opening of Genesis 32 Jacob
met angels and called the place *Mahanaim,* which
means *two camps.* Jacob knew that the angels formed
God's camp but his group was men's camp. Indeed
he had always done it his way, man's way. He knew
he stood at a crucial crossroad of his life and something drastic had to happen in order for him to leave

this place alive. He had always tried his own schemes and had prevailed. He had deceived his brother Esau twice, once for his birthright and a second time for his blessing. He had also cheated his father-in-law Laban by inventing a stratagem that would leave him with the biggest and strongest flock. We seldom see him pray or meditate as was his father's habit (Genesis 24:63) and he almost never really submitted his decisions to God for a direction in His life, but this time he found himself desperate and he prayed to the God of His fathers. He knew God's hand was upon him to bless him and indeed, in the past, the Lord had cleverly used every one of his schemes to advance His plans and purposes, but now for the first time of his life he was indubitably confronted with God's camp. He prayed a heart rending prayer of survival, reminding God of His former instruction to him:

*"Then Jacob prayed, 'O God of my father Abraham, God of my father Isaac, O LORD, who said to me, "Go back to your country and your relatives, and I will make you prosper,"' (Gen. 32:9).*

In his plea Jacob was mindful to beseech the God of his forefathers Abraham and Isaac as He was not unaware that they were those who first received the promises. Then he confessed his own unworthiness despite his success so far:

*"I am unworthy of all the kindness and faithfulness you have shown your servant. I had only my staff when I crossed this Jordan, but now I have become two groups."* (Gen. 32:10).

In verse 11 he even acknowledged his fear but he also reminded God of His promise to him and his descendants:

*"But you have said, 'I will surely make you prosper and will make your descendants like the sand of the sea, which cannot be counted.'" (Gen. 32:12).*

He knew that God could not fulfill His promise without him and his descendants so he was hoping to prevail once again, but God's response was not quite what Jacob expected and the angel of the Lord was dispatched to wrestle with him. Indeed that night there were two camps in Jacob's life but he was determined to win this confrontation as, to his understanding, it was the last chance for him and his offspring to survive.

Let us make a parenthesis here and recall Israel's situation today. At the time this book is written, Israel is under threat of destruction from Iran. Although the nations did not seem to take him too seriously, President Ahmadinejad relentlessly repeated that his goal was to destroy the Zionist state and Israel finds herself again in a precarious situation as Jacob was. So far the new Iranian government has not changed position on this matter. For the Jewish State it is a matter of survival and it is not the first time in history that the Jews find themselves cornered. This is a crucial opportunity for the people of Israel, let alone the Church, to pray, as Jacob did, for God to remember His promises. For the government of Israel the only human, political and military option is to defend the nation, even at the price of a preemptive strike on the Iranian nuclear sites. Even the thought of the destructive outcome of an eventual

Iranian nuclear attack would dwarf the world's opposition to the Israeli decision to attack first.

In Genesis 32 Jacob wrestled all night with the angel but in the course of this struggle he was injured and found himself limping. Nonetheless, he received the uttermost blessing: a change of name which in the Bible generally signifies a change of nature:

Wounded as he was, Jacob could not fight in the flesh anymore or devise any new stratagem. Now God knew that in order for Jacob to depart from Peniel in victory, he had to become a new man: Jacob *the supplanter* had to give way to the new creature, *Israel*. He couldn't act any longer in his own strength as he had so often done, but now his victory lay in this new name which the angel gave him. It was granted him neither by might nor by his own power since he was made physically weaker. As Jacob left the place, he called it Peniel for he had surely seen God in the form of a man, probably Yeshua Himself who was sending another prophetic glimpse of the future salvation and new birth of the descendants of Israel.

*"You will leave your name to my chosen ones as a curse; the Sovereign LORD will put you to death, **but to His servants He will give another name."** (Is. 65:15).*

Jacob did not have to convert to another religion to symbolically acquire this change of nature. He kept his Hebrew identity and remained the father of the twelve tribes of Israel. In many passages of scripture his old name *Jacob* is an expression of the old Jewish nature but the new name *Israel* already heralds life from the dead for the Jewish people, as it is written *"...The deliverer will come from Zion; he will turn godlessness away from Jacob. And this is my covenant with them when I take away their sins."* (Romans 11:25-26). Although today the Jewish People are called Israel in anticipation of its new nature, godlessness will have to be taken away from her and she will genuinely become *Israel* with its full spiritual implications. This will happen at the end of a long night of centuries of struggles, but as sure as the sun rose on Jacob's new life in Peniel, the fulfillment of God's promises will rise on the Jews as a nation. Some would argue that salvation is an individual choice and that it is impossible for a whole nation to be saved. Yet the verse does mention *all Israel* and we know that nothing is impossible to God. This is all the more convincing as it echoes several such prophecies from the Old Testament which Paul often quotes in his epistles. If Christians do not believe anymore that God's word is true and relevant even for today, there is no hope left. The word of God is still a light unto our path as much today as it was in Bible times.

Indeed Israel's salvation is the only real way for the Jewish people to be clothed with their genuine Jewish identity in Yeshua the Jewish Messiah. This is why Paul describes himself as *an Israelite* (Romans 11:1), but understanding the symbolism behind Jacob's change of name is crucial to discerning the prophecies concerning Israel and her call among the nations, as we will see later. As we read the Psalms and the Prophets, we may become aware of the difference between the use of Jacob and that of Israel in the text. Jacob often symbolizes the unsaved Jew whereas Israel stands for the new Jewish nature already in process today:

*"For the LORD has chosen **Jacob to be His own,** Israel to be **His treasured possession"*** (Ps. 135:4).

141

The Jews have always been a people set apart for God but they become His treasured possession when they see the one we all have pierced.

And again:

> *"Sing for joy, O heavens, for the LORD has done this; shout aloud, O earth beneath. Burst into song, you mountains, you forests and all your trees, for the LORD **has redeemed Jacob, He displays His glory in Israel.**" (Is. 44:23).*

God's glory will truly be displayed in Israel, but He will do it in stages, as we will see in the next chapter.

We see the same pattern concerning the promise of the land:

> *He remembers his covenant forever, the word he commanded, for a thousand generations, the covenant he made with Abraham, the oath he swore to Isaac. He confirmed it **to Jacob as a decree, to Israel as an everlasting covenant**: "To you I will give the land of Canaan as the portion you will inherit."*
> *Psalms 105:8-11*

Here again the difference is conspicuous. Jacob is promised the land as a decree, which presupposes the settlement of the unsaved Jews on it but the decree becomes an everlasting covenant to the Jewish nation after salvation.

This difference between Jacob and Israel is subtle but definitely present in the scriptures. Let's examine one last example, among others.

*"So they went up out of Egypt and came to their father Jacob in the land of Canaan. 26 They told him, 'Joseph is still alive! In fact, he is ruler of all Egypt.'* **Jacob was stunned; he did not believe them.**" *(Gen. 45:25-26).*

It is generally accepted that Joseph is a figure of Messiah and indeed the story of his life reflects what the rabbinical scriptures refer to as *the suffering Messiah* or *the Messiah son of Joseph*. In the verse above, it is significant that, as long as Jacob did not believe, he remained with his old name *Jacob* although the angel had already given him his new name at Peniel. On the other hand the following verses show us a different Jacob:

*But when they told him everything Joseph had said to them, and when he saw the carts Joseph had sent to carry him back, the spirit of their father Jacob revived. And* **Israel** *said, "***I'm convinced! My son Joseph is still alive***. I will go and see him before I die."* Genesis 45:27-28

It is only when Jacob's faith wakes up, when he recognizes that Joseph, symbolizing the Jewish Messiah, is still alive, that the Bible calls him *Israel*.

## God's process of restoration of and through Israel

### A–The first level of life

We see several stages of life in the scriptures and most of them are exemplified throughout the history of the Jewish people. The progression from one level to the other helps us to understand God's plan not only for Israel but also through her.

- The first level of life is very obvious, it is physical and is called in Hebrew *nishmat Haim*, which bears the root *breathing* or *soul*. It is mentioned in the following passage:

  *"The LORD God formed the man from the dust of the ground and breathed into his nostrils the breath of life, and the man became a living being." (Gen. 2:7).*

It describes the physical birth of man, the fact that man or a group of people is alive and breathes. From that moment man has a soul and is considered by God as alive, responsible for his own deeds.

### B–The second level of life

The second level is the birth of a nation and it is identified as such in the Bible as we will see in a while. One of its main characteristics is generally its establishment on a territory or land. The Concise Oxford Dictionary describes a nation as *a community of people of mainly common descent, history, language etc. forming a state or **inhabiting a territory***. We see exactly this in Ezekiel 37 and although we appreciate that this passage of scripture might be interpreted relating to the birth of the Church, it is difficult to ignore what the text explicitly says:

*"Then he said to me: 'Son of man, **these bones are the whole house of Israel**. They say, "Our bones are dried up and our hope is gone; we are cut off."' (Ezek. 37:11).*

The way God relates to these *bones* which represent Israel, stirs our curiosity: He sees this people as dry, meaning lifeless:

*"He led me back and forth among them, and I saw a great many bones on the floor of the valley, bones that were **very dry**." (Ezek. 37:2).*

God was not content with Israel having attained only the first level of life. Yes, God's people were physically alive and had a rich experience of interaction with the Lord. The Jews had already experienced both the Lord's wrath and grace many times in history, but something was missing which would make them reach a more advanced stage of life. Before using the prophet in this progression, God asks a relevant question:

*"He asked me, 'Son of man, **can these bones live?**' I said, 'O Sovereign LORD, you alone know.'" (Ezek. 37:3).*

This question was necessary to match God's miracle working power with the difficulty of the task which would raise Israel to a higher level of life. Then the process can start:

145

*Then he said to me, "Prophesy to these bones and say to them, 'Dry bones, hear the word of the LORD! This is what the Sovereign LORD says to these bones: I will make breath enter you, and you will come to life. I will attach tendons to you and make flesh come upon you and cover you with skin; I will put breath in you, and you will come to life. Then you will know that I am the LORD.'" Ezekiel 37:4-6*

These verses suggest, in a most vivid way, the establishment of Israel as a nation:

- First a noise is heard, a rattling sound suggesting the threats of war when Israel obtained the legal right to become a nation in 1948. They were weak Holocaust survivors who had hardly time to form an army. This land had been for them the embodiment of hope for so many centuries, and they were probably convinced that their troubles were left behind, when, suddenly, the *noise* broke out. Just as Sanballat and the Arabs were hostile to the building of the wall in Jerusalem in the book of Nehemiah, a coalition of Arab states welcomed them with a concerted attack expected to be a glaring major Arab victory. However, to the surprise of the whole world, in a twist of the situation, the Jews got the upper hand and this war is still known in Arabic as *Al Nakba*, the catastrophe. Judging by the fact that the Arab nations far surpassed the Jews both in armament and army size, it is not farfetched to discern God's hand in this victory. The nation of Israel was born not only through a vote in the

United Nations but by an Israeli overwhelming supremacy on the ground and Deborah's song resounded with utter relevance:

*"My heart is with Israel's princes, with the willing volunteers among the people. Praise the LORD!" (Jud. 5:9).*

And again:

*"Kings came, they fought; the kings of Canaan fought at Taanach by the waters of Megiddo, but they carried off no silver, no plunder. From the heavens the stars fought, from their courses they fought against Sisera." (Jud. 5:19:20).*

Israel gained authority over all the territories that had been agreed upon by the United Nations. The newly born Jewish state also recovered the Arab popu-lated areas of Jaffa, Ramla, the Galilee and the Negev. Nonetheless, this coordinated Arab onslaught cost many lives to Israel and poignant stories of the battles are still related today. Indeed the 1948 Israeli–Arab war that lasted over nine months was a rattling sound in the Middle East.

- Then the life-giving process evolves with the movement of the *bones*:

*"So I prophesied as I was commanded. And as I was prophesying, there was a noise, a rattling sound, **and the bones came together, bone to bone." (Ezek. 37:7).***

147

The bones come together, bone to bone, and we cannot help thinking of the different waves of Jews returning to their land from the nations. They had dispersed around the world and still had preserved their forefathers' religion and traditions. They had been aliens in so many countries and many of them had been forced to relinquish their original faith to adopt a foreign religion. They were separated by distance, language and culture but they never lost their deep sense of solidarity between them. Now they came to live together, the Poles next to the Yemenites, the Germans and Russians in proximity with those coming from the Arab world, all realizing that they were experiencing a fulfillment of the prophecies:

*"He will raise a banner for the nations and gather the exiles of Israel; He will assemble the scattered people of Judah from the four quarters of the earth." (Is. 11:12).*

This huge immigration to Israel fails to be grasped by many people as the return of the Jews to the land of their forefathers, as proclaimed long ago by the prophets. Nevertheless this exodus from the nations where they had scattered was to intensify and Israel grew to become the most modern sophisticated democracy in the Middle East. Determined and inspired by a zealous Zionism, they could overcome their cultural differences and they joined forces to dry the swamps on the Promised Land. Neither the pestilence, nor the scorching sun, nor the shortage of suitable equipment could stall their labour as they endeavoured together, bone to bone, on this tiny piece of land where they had decided to spend the rest of their lives.

In Ezekiel's prophecy, the movement of the bones to the same destination is indeed something to marvel about but it is echoed by another passage of scriptures:

> *I will surely gather all of you, O Jacob; I will surely bring together the remnant of Israel. I will bring them together like sheep in a pen, like a flock in its pasture; the place will throng with people. One who breaks open the way will go up before them; they will break through the gate and go out. Their king will pass through before them, the LORD at their head. Micah 2:12-13*

By the way, these prophecies remain to be fulfilled and are not about the return from Babylon. If needed, another passage can be quoted here:

> *Though I scatter them among the peoples, yet in distant lands they will remember me. They and their children will survive, and they will return. I will bring them back from Egypt and gather them from Assyria. I will bring them **to Gilead and Lebanon**, and there will not be room enough for them. Zechariah. 10:9-10*

Now the prophet Zechariah began his ministry in 520 BC, eighteen years after Cyrus' decree to release the Jews from Babylon was issued. So this passage foresaw a return that was yet to come to pass, but notice that in verse 10, the Jews are brought back to Lebanon, which will be part of the great Israel with enlarged borders as promised by the Lord to the Jews.

149

In any case, today the Jewish new immigrants have to overcome countless difficulties. First, they need to forsake country, culture, family, security and most often their own profession, not really knowing what lies in store for them in a new land constantly under enemy's attacks. Getting out of one's comfort zone and stepping into the unknown has often been the lot of the Jewish people from Abraham's time until today. Then they must learn a new language most needed for them to adapt to the new life and environment, Hebrew being indispensable in order to get a proper job, let alone study in university. Moreover, the new immigrant has to mingle in the melting pot of Israel and become *Israeli* both in heart and mindset. This is not an easy challenge for many who still remain with their own cultural baggage and have a propensity to prefer the proximity of those of their own background. Claiming that there are no frictions between the different cultures in Israel would be far from the truth. The Orthodox Jews from Europe have their own clan and customs. They would not even mingle with their Sepharadic brothers. The Ethiopians, the Russians, the Moroccans do their utmost to come close to the native born Israelis and indeed they have been somehow successful in this process, although much remains to be done. Great efforts have been invested not only by the Israeli governments since 1948 but also by several organizations to promote common cultural events bringing Jews and Arabs together. The nation repeats its unabashed efforts to fill the cultural gaps and facilitate a harmonious and peaceful cooperation among these diverse factions of the population.

- The tendons, the flesh and the skin suggest the different institutions and authorities which constitute a nation: a judiciary as well as an educational system, an army, a parliament, a government and all of them were birthed without any major upheaval. In a display of exemplary democracy, the judges of the Israeli Supreme Court deal equally with Israeli and Palestinian complaints in a way that would put to shame many so called democracies particularly in the Middle East. The I.D.F. (Israel Defense Forces) is a melting pot where Jews, Muslims, Christians and Druze fight side by side with the same ideal and ardour. In fact, more and more Israeli Arab Christians show their willingness to serve in the I.D.F. and defend their country side by side with other Israelis. In the media they openly declare their loyalty to the state of Israel and they are persecuted for their clear Zionist stand. The Knesset (the Israeli Parliament) is an arena where Israeli Arabs who call themselves Palestinians can be members and still use their official position to uphold Israel's fiercest enemies. Yet in the same way as the skin, the tendons and the flesh contribute to the life of the body, the Israeli elaborate institutions function successfully amidst a region where dictatorships prevail.

This process of restoration of Israel has been maturing for decades as an undeniable act of God although the world does not see it this way. Yet long ago, the Lord had promised Abraham that Israel would become a nation:

*"I will make you into a great nation and I will bless you; I will make your name great, and you will be a blessing. I will bless those who bless you, and whoever curses you I will curse; and all peoples on earth will be blessed through you." (Gen. 12:2-3).*

700 years before Yeshua came to the land this mind-blowing prophecy was echoed by the prophet Isaiah:

*Before she goes into labor, she gives birth; before the pains come upon her, she delivers a son. Who has ever heard of such a thing? Who has ever seen such things? Can a country be born in a day or a nation be brought forth in a moment? Yet no sooner is Zion in labor than she gives birth to her children. Isaiah 66:7-8*

We can pause here and wonder at the fact that, in the episode of the valley of the dry bones, God chose a mere man, Ezekiel, to be used in His plan of action. He could have achieved it by Himself in an extravagant demonstration of His glory but He preferred a man to lay the foundation of His project by an uttered prophecy. Ezekiel had access to the Lord through a vision and he was entrusted with the noble task of prophesying. Could the prophet symbolize the Church who, aware of her call toward Israel would prophetically pray the nation into existence? This is actually what took place when Christians around the world prayed for the physical restoration of the Jewish people back to their land. How utterly blessed many of them must have felt when they saw their prayers fulfilled in 1948! This is the wonder of prophecy and prayer. Man is involved from the very genesis of God's unfolding plan. Although prophecy may be blurred by many factors of time, culture and language, it is always there for the shrewd eyes and the discerning ears of the diligent believer who harkens to the Almighty God and prayerfully longs for its fulfillment. The word of God had to be proclaimed and the Holy Spirit was used in the process. It clearly reveals that the restoration of Israel as a nation was inspired and breathed by the Creator's own spirit. It also testifies to the power of genuine and God-inspired prophecy:

> *"This is what the Sovereign LORD says to these bones: I will make breath enter you, and you will come to life." (Ezek. 37:5).*

True prophecy assures us that even if its fulfillment tarries, it will surely come to pass. It is a beacon for the nations and an anchor for the believers. It is certainly not fortuitous and it accomplishes God's purpose in His appointed time.

Now that this life giving process is unfolding, it is part of Israel's growth and it undoubtedly involves the land. Ulf Ekman wrote about Israel's call:

> *"Without the land, the calling cannot be realized, and without God, the people cannot fulfill its true role. This is why, when the Lord brings restoration to His people, He begins with the land."[22]*

This stage of the restoration of Israel obviously includes the borders. If Israel is a field of preparation for the Lord's kingdom to be established from Jerusalem, the borders have to sooner or later expand to what God intends them to be at the full implementation of His plan. Accordingly, the establishment of God's kingdom on earth for 1000 years must be prepared in line with God's prerogative. This preparation includes faith in biblical borders promised by God. Similarly, to use the example of our sanctification, it would be improper and unbiblical to continue in sin, assuming that we will be suddenly and supernaturally made holy right before the Lord's return. The Bible tells us to work out our salvation with fear and trembling and become the spotless bride that God desires. This process of sanctification is necessary for us to be taken into His kingdom and progressive sanctification will ultimately bring the Church to the closest stage possible to God's will:

*"May he strengthen your hearts so that you will be blameless and holy in the presence of our God and Father when our Lord Jesus comes with all his holy ones." (1 Thes. 3:13).*

To the same degree, it would be foolish to believe that we can move the borders of Israel contrary to God's will as promised and prophesied in His word. Even if we believe that the boundaries prophesied in Ezekiel 47 are for the Millennium, we cannot take another direction and shrink the borders before the Millennium just because we hold the opinion that this choice would lead to peace. Believing and praying in line with God's perfect will is crucial to being part of His gigantic masterpiece. While there is a time for God to restore the full borders of Israel, it would be presumptuous to take a turn and relinquish the new boundaries that God gave His people as a result of the 1967 war. The present borders were not only God's gift to the Jewish state but also the groundwork for the establishment of His kingdom on earth from Jerusalem for 1000 years. Although this does not justify any Israeli invasion of territories, we ought to agree with God's plan of restoration of the biblical borders which is **in progress** and will surely attain its complete fulfillment. This may occur either in peace or through birth pains as has been the case so far.

Here again, the fact that God calls Israel dry or life-less prior to its physical restoration as a nation shows that Zionism is the groundwork for this level of life. On the other hand, anti-Zionism implies a dry, lifeless Jewish people, as the Lord qualifies it before the first breath of prophecy is blown over the bones. This is why anti-Zionism runs the danger of becoming the corridor of anti-Semitism and we can only beseech the Church not to ebb into this pitfall, but God, in His omnipotence and omnipresence, is the author and the master builder of Zionism. He is at the source of every genuine, pure biblical Zionist act on the land of Israel because His heart and holy design is for His people to have life and have it to the full. Zionism is definitely the first stage of this full-ness on this tiny piece of planet earth that He foreknew from creation. Anti-Zionism would keep the Jews trapped in the gloomy dungeons of some nations to make them easy prey to anti-Semitism. This is how they became the black sheep of Europe in history but God's cry resounds from the night of the ages: "Let My people go" so it is God who implicitly warns us against anti-Zionism.

However, the dispersion of the Jews in the nations needs to be seen as a sovereign act of God as well as a piece of His gigantic puzzle toward the full accomplishment of His will with and through His people. We already have some glimpse of this in the early history of the Jews. Even before the promise of the land was confirmed to Jacob, the decision had already fallen for the Israelites to be 400 years in Egyptian exile and slavery:

*"Then the LORD said to him, 'Know for cer-tain that your descendants will be strangers in a country not their own, and they will*

155

*be enslaved and mistreated four hundred years.'" (Gen. 15:13).*

This time the Lord's decision to send His people to Egypt was not because of the sin of Israel but it was necessary to have them confined in the agony of bondage for four centuries before He brought them to the holy land. This was the only way that was deemed fitting by the Almighty God to prevent the patriarchs and the tribes from dispersing to the rest of the world. It was God who inspired Joseph to insist that his brothers and his father Jacob come and settle in Egypt. The famine that was raging in the land of Canaan at that time was allowed by the Lord to give enough incentive to Jacob to leave the land and settle in Egypt according to His timing. This time it was God's plan to evacuate the patriarch from the Promised Land for a long season. Besides, Joseph declared, perhaps in an extraordinary prophetic way:

*"But God sent me ahead of you to preserve for you a remnant on earth and to save your lives by a great deliverance." (Gen.45:7).*

They had to endure together as one body in the same inferno of Egypt before going through the desert for 40 years and only then inherit the land. So the preservation of the Jews as a homogeneous people at the birth of the Jewish history was crucial for the rest of God's plan to develop. In fact the experience of Egypt and the wilderness took place not only to teach the people a deep lesson of faith, perseverance and obedience, but also as a glimmering sign of the costly price that the people of God would have to pay in order to move from one stage of life to the other. Besides, as we can see in Ezekiel 47, before the Bible mentions the extent of the promised borders, it starts with the description of the prophet's gradual advance into the river coming from the temple:

*As the man went eastward with a measuring line in his hand, he measured off a thousand cubits and then led me through water that was ankle-deep. He measured off another thousand cubits and led me through water that was knee-deep. He measured off another thousand and led me through water that was up to the waist. He measured off another thousand, but now it was a river that I could not cross, because the water had risen and was deep enough to swim in — a river that no one could cross. He asked me, "Son of man, do you see this?" Then he led me back to the bank of the river. Ezekiel 47:3-6*

This progression is typical of the way God acts with Israel in her restoration process. It graduates from one level of blessing and anointing to the next one and every level requires a necessary degree of trust and faith. This faith can find its source in the God of Abraham, Isaac and Jacob, the same God who has driven the Jewish people through Egypt, the wandering in the desert, the different exiles and the wars of Israel. His plan is still in progress.

## C—The third level of life

*"I looked, and tendons and flesh appeared on them and skin covered them, but there was no breath in them." (Ezek. 37:8).*

157

Life as a nation was certainly a decisive and important step forward for the nation of Israel but this verse shows us that God was still not satisfied: *there was no breath in them*. Now He called the prophet to prophesy to the breath:

> *"Then he said to me, 'Prophesy to the breath; prophesy, son of man, and say to it, "This is what the Sovereign LORD says: Come from the four winds, O breath, and breathe into these slain, that they may live."' (Ezek. 37:9).*

The one thing they needed was life in the spirit, and this is the need of Israel as a nation today: the spiritual restoration of the Jewish people. It is the stage when the spirit of man is touched by God's spirit and he is born again in salvation. We see this stage of life clearly in the following verse:

> *"because through Christ Jesus the law of* **the Spirit of life** *set me free from the law of sin and death." (Rom. 8:2).*

This is evoked prophetically in the following verses:

> *"So I prophesied as he commanded me, and breath entered them; they came to life and stood up on their feet — a vast army." (Ezek. 37:10).*

It is only after Israel receives the spirit of God that she can become *a very very great army* according to the Hebrew text.

This is what the apostle Paul prayed in anguish of heart:

*I speak the truth in Christ — I am not lying, my conscience confirms it in the Holy Spirit — I have great sorrow and unceasing anguish in my heart. For I could wish that I myself were cursed and cut off from Christ **for the sake of my brothers, those of my own race, the people of Israel.** Theirs is the adoption as sons; theirs the divine glory, the covenants, the receiving of the law, the temple worship and the promises. Theirs are the patriarchs, and from them is traced the human ancestry of Christ, who is God over all, forever praised! Amen. Romans 9:1-5*

Although the rabbis don't have the same conception of salvation as we believers in Yeshua have, they do believe in the Gehula, the perfection of all things and peace not only for His people but for the whole world. Then will the words of the prophet Isaiah be fulfilled:

*"The infant will play near the hole of the cobra, and the young child put his hand into the viper's nest. They will neither harm nor destroy on all my holy mountain, for the earth will be full of the knowledge of the LORD as the waters cover the sea." (Isaiah 11:8-9).*

This peace which, as we know, is linked to a complete change of nature, is the ultimate Jewish hope and even in the secular circles numerous songs express this deep longing. However the Lord makes clear to Ezekiel that this salvation can happen only with a blow of His spirit and here again it takes place with the direct intervention of a mere man, the prophet. However this third stage of life couldn't come without or before the second. Israel needs first to be born as a nation (Isaiah 66:7-9) in order for the Holy Spirit to start his work of salvation in a wider and deeper way. As a matter of fact, the process of revelation of Yeshua as the Jewish Messiah to the Jews did not start before the return of the Jewish people to the land in 1948. It was only in the early sixties that the first Jewish Messianic fellowships sprang up in Israel as well as many other nations. This reality truly reflects the order of the different sequences that took place in the valley of the dry bones, but long ago, several men of God already understood that the fulfillment of the physical and spiritual restoration of the Jews was only a question of time. One of the most read of his time was Spurgeon who boldly declared:

*The hour is approaching, when the tribes shall go up to their own country; when Judea, so long a howling wilderness, shall once more blossom like the rose; when, if the temple itself be not restored, yet on Zion's hill shall be raised some Christian building, where the chants of solemn praise shall be heard as erst of the old Psalms of David were sung in the Tabernacle . . . I think we do not attach sufficient importance to the restoration of the Jews. We do not think enough about it. But certainly, if there is anything promised in the Bible it is this. I imagine that you cannot read the Bible without seeing clearly that there is to be an actual restoration of the Children of Israel . . . For when the Jews are restored, the fullness of the Gentiles shall be gathered in; and as soon as they return, then Jesus will come upon Mount Zion with his ancients gloriously, and the halcyon days*

*of the millennium shall then dawn; we shall*
*then know every man to be a brother and a*
*friend; Christ shall rule with universal sway.[23]*

Again God's order in His restoration of Israel shows that Zionism is a precondition of the salvation of the Jews as a nation. In fact we could almost hazard to state that the gradual development of Zionism on the ground and the progressive recovery of the biblical borders by Israel are triggering the salvation of more Jewish souls–the revelation of Yeshua as the true Messiah to the Jewish nation. It was after the extension of Israel's borders and the unification of Jerusalem in 1967 that the Messianic Body of Messiah in Israel was born; it then grew and developed. This process will continue until the Jews become *a very very great army* of Jewish believers in Yeshua. The Bible always astounds us with prophecies whose magnitude challenges both the Jewish and Christian mind. Even today, many would have a hard time believing that a revival of souls can take place in the holy land, almost 2000 years after Yeshua drew crowds behind him and the apostles saw thousands come to receive the true Jewish Messiah in their hearts. Yet the Spirit of the Lord was promised to fall upon this land of Israel and these bones will actually come to life as the prophet Zachariah announced it in days of old.

*And I will pour out on the house of David and*
*the inhabitants of Jerusalem a spirit of grace*
*and supplication. They will look on me, the*
*one they have pierced, and they will mourn*
*for him as one mourns for an only child, and*
*grieve bitterly for him as one grieves for a*
*firstborn son. On that day the weeping in*
*Jerusalem will be great, like the weeping of*

161

*Hadad Rimmon in the plain of Megiddo. The land will mourn, each clan by itself, with their wives by themselves: the clan of the house of David and their wives, the clan of the house of Nathan and their wives, the clan of the house of Levi and their wives, the clan of Shimei and their wives, and all the rest of the clans and their wives. Zechariah 12:10-14*

This prophecy is yet to be fulfilled and speaks of a glorious time to come when the Jews genuinely repent in weeping and mourning. It will be an overwhelming realization of 2000 years of Jewish rejection of the redeemer who came to live amidst His people upon the land and was not identified, even by the Pharisees who were supposed to be versed in the Holy Scriptures. It will be a total surrender of a nation deeply in search of the truth. The Lord will respond to this quest by sending His Spirit of grace and supplication that alone can open the eyes of the blind and the hearts of the unbelieving. In the passage above, the picture of the separation between men and their wives is typical of a Jewish Orthodox mourning, which makes this outstanding prophecy even more ambitious, particularly when we know the obstinate refutation of the Christian message within the Jewish Orthodox circles today. However, this prophecy is inexorably unfolding in our present age and its complete fulfillment will surely come to pass.

Notice that this extraordinary event will take place in the land and among the families of this people. This is a meaningful answer to those who hold the opinion that Israel can or will be saved without the need of a land and without being born as a nation. There is a sequence of events which need to take place before the coming of the Lord:

*"He must remain in heaven until the time comes for God to restore everything, as he promised long ago through his holy prophets." (Acts 3:21).*

It is undeniable that the prophets of old foresaw the return of the Jewish people to the land as a nation and the outpouring of the Holy Spirit upon all flesh before the Lord's coming:

*And it shall come to pass afterward That I will pour out My Spirit on all flesh; Your sons and your daughters shall prophesy, your old men shall dream dreams, your young men shall see visions. And also on My menservants and on My maidservants I will pour out My Spirit in those days. Joel 2:28-29 (NKJV)*

This verse comes toward the end of a chapter which first expands on the restoration of Israel upon the land, so the order of events remains intact.

In the fifth chapter of the book of Joshua it is remarkable that the Israelites are circumcised only after they start to settle upon the land:

*Now when all the Amorite kings west of the Jordan and all the Canaanite kings along the coast heard how the LORD had dried up the Jordan before the Israelites until we had crossed over, their hearts melted and they no longer had the courage to face the Israelites. At that time the LORD said to Joshua, "Make flint knives and circumcise the Israelites again." So Joshua made flint knives and circumcised the Israelites at Gibeath Haaraloth. Joshua 5:1-3*

If we symbolically consider circumcision as a change of heart we understand that the the Jews had to first conquer the land and then be circumcised. The Old Testament shows us the link between the recovery of the land and the salvation of the people in subtle ways. We can see this as a pattern projected into the future and destiny of Israel, as circumcision of the heart is always the sign of a new nature, in this case, the salvation of the Jews.

The Israelites who were circumcised were those who believed God's solemn promise of the land to their forefathers:

*All the people that came out had been circumcised, but all the people born in the desert during the journey from Egypt had not. The Israelites had moved about in the desert forty years until all the men who were of military age when they left Egypt had died, since they had not obeyed the LORD. For the LORD had sworn to them that they would not see the land that he had solemnly promised their fathers to give us, a land flowing with milk and honey. So he raised up their sons in their place, and these were the ones Joshua circumcised. They were still uncircumcised because they had not been circumcised on the way. And after the whole nation had been circumcised, they remained where they were in camp until they were healed. Josh 5:5-8*

Here again physical circumcision is symbolical of a true circumcision of the Jewish heart heralded for the end times, but it is only after the access of the Israelites to the land that God wipes out their sins, so to speak:

*"Then the LORD said to Joshua, 'Today I have rolled away the reproach of Egypt from you.' So the place has been called Gilgal to this day." (Jos. 5:9).*

Again, what comes next is symbolic of the true Passover Lamb to be revealed in the end times, following the establishment of Israel as a nation:

*On the evening of the fourteenth day of the month, while camped at Gilgal on the plains of Jericho, the Israelites celebrated the Passover. The day after the Passover, that very day, they ate some of the produce of the land: unleavened bread and roasted grain. The manna stopped the day after they ate this food from the land; there was no longer any manna for the Israelites, but that year they ate of the produce of Canaan. Joshua 5:10-12*

Here we can see how the celebration of the Passover Lamb is closely linked to the settling down of the Israelites upon the Promised Land but the order remains the same in prophecy: first the inheritance of the land and then the spiritual restoration of the people as Ezekiel wrote it clearly in the following verses:

*"For I will take you out of the nations; I will gather you from all the countries and **bring you back into your own land.** I will sprinkle clean water on you, and you will be clean; I*

*will cleanse you from all your impurities and from all your idols." (Ezek. 36:24-25)*

It was God's plan to first prepare a country for the people and then cover it with His Spirit in the same way as He ordered the building of the temple to fill it with His presence.

The parallel seen today between the return of the Jews to the land, the growth of the nation and the coming salvation is echoed in Isaiah's prophecy:

*But now listen, O Jacob, my servant, Israel, whom I have chosen. This is what the LORD says — he who made you, who formed you in the womb, and who will help you: Do not be afraid, O Jacob, my servant, Jeshurun, whom I have chosen. **For I will pour water on the thirsty land**, and streams on the dry ground; **I will pour out my Spirit on your offspring**, and my blessing on your descendants. **They will spring up like grass in a meadow, like poplar trees by flowing streams.** Isaiah 44:1-4*

This outstanding outpouring of the Holy Spirit takes place specifically upon the land at a time of spiritual thirst and it is at that time that the Jewish people becomes "a very very great army". An army's task is to fight and win a war, it has a goal and indeed Israel has not lost her vision. This leads us to her fourth level of life.

### D–The fourth level of life

In their hearts, the Jews have always carried the mission to be the light of the nations as heralded by the prophet Isaiah:

166

> *"See, darkness covers the earth and thick darkness is over the peoples, but the LORD rises upon you and his glory appears over you. **Nations will come to your light**, and kings to the brightness of your dawn."* (Is. 60:2-3).

This call to be a light to the world will step Israel into her fourth stage of life, although the Jews do not entirely discern what really lies behind it.

Already some great men of God saw the call of Israel from afar. Back in 1855 Charles Spurgeon preached an amazing sermon forecasting the destiny of the Jewish people:

> *For when the Jews are restored, then the fullness of the Gentiles shall be gathered in; and as soon as they return, then Jesus will come upon Mount Zion to reign with his ancients gloriously, and the halcyon days of the Millennium shall then dawn; we shall then know every man to be a brother and a friend; Christ shall rule, with universal sway.*[24]

This Jewish mission will not bring glory to Israel but to the Lord, and this is one of the main causes for His hand of protection and blessing upon His people:

> *"The wild animals honor me, the jackals and the owls, because I provide water in the desert and streams in the wasteland, to give drink to my people, my chosen, the people I formed for myself that they may proclaim my praise."* (Is. 43:20-21).

The nations are supposed to see how God can choose one of the least of the nations of the earth, remain faithful to it despite its recurring sins and transform it into a righteous nation:

> *For Zion's sake I will not keep silent, for Jerusalem's sake I will not remain quiet, till her righteousness shines out like the dawn, her salvation like a blazing torch. The nations will see your righteousness, and all kings your glory; you will be called by a new name that the mouth of the LORD will bestow. Isaiah 62:1-2*

The nations will see righteousness in Zion and will glorify the Lord, but this comes through the obstinate intercession of the prophet (verse 1) who is given as an example to every true intercessor whose burden is to pray according to God's heart desire.

While it is theoretically true that the State of Israel could be threatened by another exodus of the Jews back to the nations of the world, the present recovery of the land is different from the historical ones inasmuch as it marks the inception of the salvation of the nation, the remnant which was prophesied about so long ago. David Brickner wrote:

> *Could present-day Israel be uprooted once again from the Land because of her unbelief? I would have to say yes, though I hope not. There is a growing remnant of believers in Jesus in the land of Israel, and God has consistently extended mercy on behalf of the remnant of his people. Paul makes much of the theology of the remnant in asserting*

*that God has not forsaken his people. The church can rejoice in that ever-increasing remnant, with all the ramifications it holds for the modern and future state of Israel.*[25]

However, the growth of the Body of Jewish believers does not have ramifications only for the modern Jewish state but also for the whole world. This is where we need to examine some prophecies in the light of the distinction made in an earlier chapter between Jacob and Israel:

*"In days to come **Jacob** will take root, **Israel** will bud and blossom and **fill all the world with fruit.**" (Is. 27:6).*

In this verse we see the three last levels of life:

- *Jacob will take root* corresponds to the second level, life as a nation upon the land.
- *Israel will bud and blossom* points at the third level, life of in the spirit as believers in Yeshua.
- *...and fill all the world with fruit* refers to Israel's call to the nations.

Please notice in this verse that it is *Jacob*, still unsaved, who comes to settle upon the land but it is *Israel* who, after receiving the revelation of the truth in Yeshua, is entrusted to bring fruit to the whole world. Paul's prayer for the Israelites was beyond just the salvation of an ancient people. The apostle knew that the salvation of the Jews was but another step in what God had planned for His people from the foundation of the world:

*"God did not reject his people, **whom he foreknew**. Don't you know what the Scripture*

*says in the passage about Elijah — how he appealed to God against Israel" (Rom. 11:2).*

By the word *foreknew* Paul assumed that God initiated with this people something which He must complete. Further on Paul depicts the magnitude of God's purpose through the Jewish nation:

*"Now if their fall is riches for the world, and their failure riches for the Gentiles, how much more their fullness!" (Rom. 11:12, NKJV).*

This verse shows us that something even better than the present progress of salvation on the planet is to be expected when, and not if, the Jews are saved. In this chapter Paul compares the blindness of the Jewish people to some kind of death but not a terminal one. It is a death awaiting resurrection, a new life, not for the Jews only but for the benefit of the nations:

*"For if their being cast away is the reconciling of the world, what will their acceptance be but life from the dead?" (Rom. 11:15, NKJV).*

In his book "Jacob I have loved" Lance Lambert wrote:

*"The purpose of God was that Jacob should possess the land, should become a people, should be a blessing"[26]*

In the past the Church had a message of blessing for Jacob, but as Israel is getting saved, time has come for the Jews to bless the nations. It took almost 2000 years for the message of the gospel brought by the Church missionaries to take root in the Jewish heart.

Before that, the veil stayed upon Jacob's eyes so that he remained attached to, and perhaps also blinded by rabbinical tradition and interpretation of the Old Testament. This had the advantage of keeping the Jews alive as a people for so many centuries, and our Jewish identity remained intact, but when the Holy Spirit revealed to them the message of the Gospel in the Old Testament, many Jews accepted the truth that the Christians retained for 2000 years. This might have caused some pride and excessive triumphalism within the Church and both the Church and the Messianic Jews need now much humility so that God's plan might be fulfilled in and through them. This plan is for Israel to *cover the world with fruit* (Isaiah 27:6) and this process is already at work:

> *"The LORD will have compassion on Jacob; once again he will choose Israel and will settle them in their own land. Aliens will join them and unite with the house of Jacob."* *(Is. 14:1).*

We see several points in this verse:
- *He will have a compassion on Jacob*:
This is marked by the return of the Jews to their land as a nation within the present borders. For the last 2000 years the Jews had consistently prayed: *next year in Jerusalem*, but now this dream has come true, not because we deserved it but because of God's unfathomable grace and compassion.

- *Again He will choose Israel and will settle them in their own land*:
In God's eyes the completion of this return to the land is when the biblical borders are retrieved and the

Jews from all over the world can settle on the precise location and territory which God had solemnly promised our forefathers.

*- Aliens will join them and unite to the house of Jacob*:
This predicts the collapse of the wall of partition which has stood so adamantly between the Jews and the Church. Indeed Paul referred to this with great expectation:

> *For He himself is our peace, who has made the two one and has destroyed the barrier, the dividing wall of hostility, by abolishing in his flesh the law with its commandments and regulations. His purpose was to create in himself one new man out of the two, thus making peace, and in this one body to reconcile both of them to God through the cross, by which he put to death their hostility. Ephesians 2:14-16*

However we had to wait 2000 years for the appearance of two decisive elements as the first signs of this fulfillment:
- First, the salvation of the Jews had to be birthed and produce the Messianic Body of Messiah.

- Then the Church, or at least part of it, and the Messianic Jews had to start working through their divergences although this is indeed an ongoing process with many obstacles and stumbling blocks on the way, but it is crucial for the Church to acknowledge her need to accept spiritual nourishment from the Jewish olive tree:

*If some of the branches have been broken off, and you, though a wild olive shoot, have been grafted in among the others and now **share in the nourishing sap from the olive root,** do not boast over those branches. If you do, consider this: You do not support the root, **but the root supports you.** Romans 11:17-18*

Unfortunately, for centuries the Church has systematically uprooted herself from any Jewish root to the point that a great part of it today remains almost entirely ignorant of the Jewish foundations of the Christian faith. Yet these foundations prevailed in the first Church of the Book of Acts. We often tend to forget that the apostles taught and preached the Gospel out of the Old Testament with a Jewish mindset and, to some measure, not relinquishing biblical Jewish traditions. Unfortunately the early Church of Rome meticulously proceeded to eliminate anything that was deemed as *judaizing* and some decisions taken by the Council of Laodicea in the fourth century were just some more axes smiting at the roots of the Christian faith. Although it would be too long and perhaps off track to expand on this topic in this book, it is necessary to remind ourselves of at least one quotation from the Council of Laodicea:

*Christians shall not Judaize and be idle on Saturday, the Sabbath, but shall work on that day; but the Lord's day (Sunday) they shall especially honor, and, as being Christians, shall, if possible, do no work on that day. If, however, they are found Judaizing, they shall be shut out from Christ.*[27]

It is on the background of such a mindset that the Church of Rome equally decided to change the date of the Passover celebration and the name of the feast became Easter, after the goddess Astarte. Although these decisions might be considered trivial, they are of doctrinal importance and were in direct contradiction with the doctrine of the apostles in the first church in Jerusalem. This does not necessarily mean that the Church should now automatically return to the original ecclesiastic patterns. However, it is enriching to understand for instance *why*, for the first Messianic Church in Jerusalem, the Sabbath day had to be the seventh day of the week, *why* the feast of Passover had received such a name and *why* it was important to understand the underlying reasons of its original date. These important points along with many others have more to do with the core of the Gospel than with Jewish tradition. Indeed the early Church of Rome had many opponents, especially among those who had remained faithful to the apostles' teaching, but they were systematically persecuted until they almost disappeared from the Christian scene. Yet a time is coming when Zechariah's prophecy will gradually be fulfilled:

> *"This is what the LORD Almighty says: 'In those days ten men from all languages and nations will take firm hold of one Jew by the hem of his robe and say, "Let us go with you, because we have heard that God is with you."'" (Zech. 8:23).*

This is a staggering prophecy that is generally not taught from the pulpit in churches because it is mind blogging for preachers who cannot cope with the idea that anything good would come out of the Jewish people in the future. They still profoundly believe that the Jews have been rejected and the whole truth remains now monopolized by the Church. To them the synagogue will always remain portrayed by the statue of the blindfolded woman still standing on the front of the Strasbourg cathedral in France: why would the nations follow this woman who has persisted for so long in denying the truth, the way and the life? What can she bring to the nations that they would want to follow her? Nonetheless, the missing link to understanding the *why* and the *when* lies in the revelation of Yeshua to the Jews. Once they had zeal but no knowledge, but a time is coming when they will remain animated by the same zeal armed with profound knowledge. The Jewish sages had searched the scriptures with such earnestness and the scribes had compiled them scrupulously, but they needed the missing pearl of truth, Yeshua as their Jewish Messiah. The discovery of this truth will make their faith pure, whole and, at that point, they will be able to bring the Church and the nations the very roots that had been lost long ago. Still there is much more that will come from the original olive tree and we can only see part of the whole picture, but one day many more of these spiritual pearls will be unveiled for the benefit and the edifying of the nations.

Yet we are still curiously challenged by the following question: what riches can the Jews bring to the nations in the end times? To answer this we must first bear in mind that, although the Jewish people suffered the curse of persecutions, they have always carried with them the Lord's blessings in many spheres of life. Their obvious propensity to become illustrious in science, music, literature and finances, has made them very successful and has indeed opened many doors to them in many nations. Their intelligence in high technology, especially in the medical sphere but not only, has been a blessing to many people in the world. The traditional Passover Jewish song *Dayenu* would thoroughly apply to these qualities. *Dayenu* means *it would have been enough for us*, but these talents, as useful and edifying as they may be, will be dwarfed by the fulfillment of the Lord's spiritual call for the Jews. God intends to give them a spiritual wisdom that would complete the knowledge of the Church and make the two perfectly complementary. Let us examine some specific elements which have been abandoned by the Church and are so missing to her faith:

> *For I could wish that I myself were cursed and cut off from Christ for the sake of my brothers, those of my own race, the people of Israel. Theirs is the adoption as sons; theirs the divine glory, the covenants, the receiving of the law, the temple worship and the promises. Theirs are the patriarchs, and from them is traced the human ancestry of Christ, who is God over all, forever praised! Amen. Romans 9:3-5*

There are seven items mentioned in verse 4 and 5 and the eighth one is their crown: Yeshua. This last item is the only one that the Jews have been missing for 2000 years, but once Yeshua is accepted as Saviour, their faith relies on the sure milestones which the Church is so severely in need of. For instance, it is inconceivable to understand *the divine glory* without studying it in the light of numerous Old Testament episodes on which the rabbis can shed at least some historical light, especially after they receive a revelation of their Jewish Saviour. Besides, several interesting historical anecdotes related in the rabbinical scriptures can be biblically filtered and can be most enriching. The Jewish scribes had compiled hundreds of events that can have a genuine historical value and can be considered quite congruent with biblical passages. It is also quite rewarding to weigh Yeshua's parables in the light of the oral law and the customs of the epoch.

Another interesting item in Paul's list is *the covenants* and their succession. While the Church generally believes that the New Covenant completely replaced the Old, the modern Jewish Body of Messiah can bring very sobering thoughts about this topic without being necessarily paradoxical to Christian theology. Similarly some Christians, having completely rejected the law, find themselves in a dilemma with **some** moral commandments and other minor laws which would enlighten and improve our moral and social life. The Messianic Body will apparently, as it is hinted in Ezekiel 8:23, receive a fresh revelation to convey these truths to the nations and specifically to Christianity.

Thank God some Christian scholars have been richly rewarded by the study of the temple worship (Romans 9:4) but it is not a secret that many teachers would not even dig into this subject under the pretense that the temple worship is not for this dispensation any longer. The rabbinical scriptures offer a vast treasure of knowledge on this theme which can be of significant interest especially if we believe that the temple depicted by the Prophet Ezekiel will actually exist in the Millennium, probably in order to exemplify the centrality of Yeshua in all the sacrifices and radiate the depth of the gospel to the nations.

One of the last items in Romans 9:4-5 is *the promises*. The theme of the land has been ignored by the Church at large for centuries perhaps because of a basic misunderstanding of the nature of God's promises to Israel, and we could affirm that the same misunderstanding affects the theme of the patriarchs.

The Messiah Yeshua, depicted by Paul as Jewish, is rarely preached in the Church worldwide as if it were a taboo topic because of its presumed irrelevancy today. However, the fact that Paul mentioned it in the 9th chapter of his epistle to the Romans, combined with the rebirth of the Jewish Messianic Church in Israel nowadays, makes it very pertinent to the fulfillment of end time prophecies. Instead, the Church has in history consistently depicted Yeshua as sandy-haired with blue eyes. This was the way He was portrayed by illustrious painters and this is still how He appears on the pages of numerous editions of children Bibles. For the average Christian mindset, to imagine a Messiah with a Jewish profile can be very challenging if not extremely galling. Consequently the Church has lost the profound implications of Yeshua's Jewish nature both in doctrine and in simple understanding of His message, especially for the end time.

These items evoked by Paul in Romans 9 are not the only ones which have been hidden from the Church. Because of the tendency to minimize the importance of whole passages from the written law, Christianity has been deprived of the feasts of the Lord and has been led by the early fathers of the Church of Rome to invent a new terminology separating the so-called *Jewish feasts* from the *Christian feasts*. This trend has persisted for many centuries under the influence of a growing anti-Semitic spirit in Europe and has introduced new festivals, often based on pagan celebrations, while suppressing some of the original biblical feasts. For instance, as mentioned above, the nations will need to come to redeemed Jerusalem every year at the Feast of Tabernacles with the threat of a curse upon their land if they do not obey this instruction. This tells us that this feast will have to be somehow related to the nations and mainly to the Church. It is sad that the deep message of the Feast of Tabernacles has been hidden to the Body of Christ for so long. Moreover, because of the Roman decision to adopt the Roman and then Gregorian calendar instead of the biblical lunar one, the dates of the feasts were altered. All this led to a significant distortion of the spiritual message of the feasts of the Lord, let alone their prophetic dimension.

With all these missing links in the Church, and the above items are far from being comprehensive, it is not accidental that Christians have lost sight of the call of Israel in God's plan and the biblical concept of the land in relation with modern Israel. Yet the Lord in His unparalleled love for His Church, has kept the Jewish people alive and is gradually taking the veil off their eyes to bless the Body of Christ with the unequalled riches that was lost across the twenty centuries of its existence. The Jews have freely received the revelation of Yeshua from the Christians but they are now entrusted with a profound message for the world:

> *"Surely you will summon nations you know not, and nations that do not know you will hasten to you, because of the LORD your God, the Holy One of Israel, for he has endowed you with splendor." (Is. 55:5).*

However, Yeshua's second coming and the resurrection of the dead are perhaps the main reasons why it is so dear in God's heart for both the Jews and the Christians to join in the fulfillment of His plan. Paul described this as *life from the dead* (Rom. 11:15) which

179

implies that the fulfillment of this fourth level of life will herald the end of this present age and the Lord's second advent.

There are many other yet unknown reasons why the ten Gentiles from the nations will seek to follow a Jew, but some of them will remain veiled until the Holy Spirit reveals them and endows the Messianic Jews a full realization of their responsibility in the fulfillment of Zechariah 8:23. However, as mentioned above, the need of humility cannot be enough emphasized on the part of both Christians and Jews for, in their complementary relation, they bear the crucial task of bringing their riches to a spiritually impoverished world in a final joint venture. In fact, although not yet applied, this concept is not completely foreign to conventional Judaism and has been often expressed by some prominent rabbis.

However, in order to assume their call it is necessary for the Jews to experience the three preceding stages of life. This is why the confirmation of Israel as a nation, the settlement of the Jews on the Promised Land and their salvation should be daily present in Christian prayers. This Jewish mission will contribute to pave the way for God's bride into His kingdom. In his book *Enter the rest* Israel Harel wrote:

> *"The people of Israel were to make it possible to catch a glimpse of the kingdom of God as it existed – His spiritual kingdom invading earth. This form of government was to be a kind of bridgehead of the kingdom of heaven on earth."*[28]

This glimpse could be conveyed only by the Jewish people who had been gifted with such blissful revelations. Their relationship with the King of the universe is basic to understanding God's interaction with His creation. Contrarily to what some may think, Israel's call is in no way annulled by the extent of her waywardness and it remains as valid as ever; the apostle Paul was well aware of it:

> As far as the gospel is concerned, they are enemies on your account; but as far as **election** is concerned, they are loved on account of the patriarchs, **for God's gifts and his call are irrevocable.** Just as you who were at one time disobedient to God have now received mercy as a result of their disobedience. Romans 11:28-30

It is never too late for God to achieve His plan through His people and the prophet Isaiah saw it from afar:

> Listen to me, O house of Jacob, all you who remain of the house of Israel, you whom I have upheld since you were conceived, and have carried since your birth. **Even to your old age and gray hairs** I am he, I am he who will sustain you. I have made you and I will carry you; I will sustain you and I will rescue you. Isaiah 46:3-4

The Jews are generally aware that their biblical responsibility to be a light to the nations depends on their establishment as a people on their own land, but the enemy of God's plan, the devil is doing his utmost to undermine this awareness and this is why he so fiercely opposes their settlement in Israel within God given borders. He knows that this third stage of life would lead God's people to enter the fourth: their call toward the nations. Yet as God enfolds His plan, He shows both Israel and the nations that there is no peace process possible outside of His sovereign will.

### The nations and the Church regarding Israel's call
God gives every nation the right and indeed the privilege to participate actively, to a huge extent in His plan for and through Israel, but what the world generally tends to ignore is that the Lord watches every one of the nations' steps regarding the Jewish nation. Every time that a decision needs to be taken concerning the State of Israel, every nation has to pronounce itself through a vote in the United Nations. As a matter of fact, in 1948 the U.N. actually divided the land of Israel by giving it boundaries which were not aligned with God's word. These are the so-called pre-1967 borders which are advanced by the nations whenever a peace process is resumed by the parties involved in the conflict. The nations are responsible for this division much more before the Lord of all the earth than they are before Israel, but it is never too late to fix this error. There can and should be some repentance accompanied with restitution. The prophecies tell us that this restitution will eventually take place with or without the nations' participation for God is as jealous for His word and plan as He was in times of old.

In the United Nations every people on the face of the globe must officially express its position on the Jewish state, not only before the world and the media but also before God. This is why it is highly important to pray for the leaders in authority in our respective nation, for the kings, the presidents, the prime and foreign affairs ministers and even the municipal leaders. In the Bible we can see how the Lord reveals His plan to some foreign pagan kings:

*In the first year of Cyrus king of Persia, **in order to fulfill the word of the LORD spoken by Jeremiah, the LORD moved the heart of Cyrus king of Persia** to make a proclamation throughout his realm and to put it in writing: "This is what Cyrus king of Persia says: "'The LORD, the God of heaven, **has given me all the kingdoms of the earth and he has appointed me to build a temple for him at Jerusalem in Judah.** Anyone of his people among you — may the LORD his God be with him, and let him go up.'"* 2 Chronicles 36:22-23*

It is far from impossible for the Lord to work in the hearts of nations leaders and plant in them a burden for the people and the land of Israel. When the enemies of Israel threaten the land by war, many Israelis cry out to the Lord because they know He has always shown Himself faithful to His people. See how King Jehoshaphat pleaded before the Lord when attacked by the Moabites, the Ammonites and the Meunites who had come to take over the land:

*But now here are men from Ammon, Moab and Mount Seir, whose territory you would not allow Israel to invade when they came from Egypt; so they turned away from them and did not destroy them. See how they are repaying us by coming to drive us **out of the possession you gave us as an inheritance.** O our God, will you not judge them?*

183

*For we have no power to face this vast army that is attacking us. We do not know what to do, but our eyes are upon you." 2 Chronicles 20:10-12*

Jehoshaphat reminded God of His promise and his prayer was answered:

*He said: "Listen, King Jehoshaphat and all who live in Judah and Jerusalem! This is what the LORD says to you: 'Do not be afraid or discouraged because of this vast army.* **For the battle is not yours, but God's.** *Tomorrow march down against them. They will be climbing up by the Pass of Ziz, and you will find them at the end of the gorge in the Desert of Jeruel.* **You will not have to fight this battle. Take up your positions; stand firm and see the deliverance the LORD will give you,** *O Judah and Jerusalem. Do not be afraid; do not be discouraged. Go out to face them tomorrow, and the LORD will be with you.'" 2 Chronicles 20:15-17*

Let us remember that at least one intercessor, Daniel, had prayed three times a day while still in exile in Babylon. There may have been more intercessors who prayed with him along the same lines. So the Lord can summon today's leaders in authority to accomplish His will regarding Israel. This can be very relevant if we think of interceding for our government. When somebody has a negative stand against Israel he is responsible for it, but when it is the position of the government of a nation through a decision taken sovereignly, the whole nation can be under a curse. In this case, the intercessors have to intervene at least in prayer. We saw in many countries how intercession could change the attitude of their leaders or even replace them. After all, we are obligated to pray for our authorities and we have good biblical reasons to believe that the Lord will accept our intercession, all the more if it is related to Israel. This is perhaps the best way to bless Israel and be blessed. Unfortunately many world leaders do not realize that they are actually cursing Israel in God's eyes by their decision regarding the Jewish state. In fact according to God's word we can either bless or curse Israel, there is biblically no indifferent option. Nonetheless God had already warned the nations about it and this warning remains relevant:

> *"On that day, when all the nations of the earth are gathered against her, I will make Jerusalem an immovable rock for all the nations. All who try to move it will injure themselves. On that day I will strike every horse with panic and its rider with madness,"* declares the LORD. *"I will keep a watchful eye over the house of Judah, but I will blind all the horses of the nations." Zechariah 12:3-4*

In the future, if such an attack is launched against the Jewish state, it may be because the Lord will have added more territory to Israel. Since we can obviously see in these verses on which side God would stand, it is important for the Christian intercessors to lift their leaders in prayer before they make the serious mistake to participate in the attack. For instance King Cyrus was actually aware that he had come to such a position for such a time as this *to build a temple for Him at Jerusalem in Judah* (as quoted above in 2 Chronicles

36:23). We can pray for a revelation of God's love for Israel. It was this insight that the queen of Sheba apparently received from the Lord:

> *Praise be to the LORD your God, who has delighted in you and placed you on his throne as king to rule for the LORD your God. **Because of the love of your God for Israel** and his desire to uphold them forever, he has made you king over them, to maintain justice and righteousness. 2 Chronicles 9:8*

The lord's intention has always been to draw the attention of the nations to the way He dealt with Israel either for blessing or for discipline. Israel is often used by God to convey crucial messages to the peoples of the earth. For instance whenever He gives Israel the victory over her enemies, it is for the nations to take heed and understand where He stands:

> *Now when all the Amorite kings west of the Jordan and all the Canaanite kings along the coast **heard how the LORD** had dried up the Jordan before the Israelites until we had crossed over, **their hearts melted** and they no longer had the courage to face the Israelites. Joshua 5:1*

We saw this in 1967 when the Egyptians ran away barefooted from the battlefield. The fact that Israel could get the upper hand against such a coalition of enemies in just six days is in itself an act of God's will. Yet God knew that this war would not only give Israel the victory but would also add more territories to the Jewish state, something which is contested today not only by most of the nations and also by many Christians . Did God make a mistake by helping the Israeli army in 1948, 1956, 1967, 1973 and onward? This is what many people are trying to insinuate. So today, if only for a moment the United Nations really wanted to know where God stands in the Middle East conflict, they should consider the fact that Israel won all the past wars since its establishment as a nation. This is clear evidence that He never wanted to give His land and His people in to the hands of the Israel's enemies:

*"For the LORD your God is the one who goes with you to fight for you against your enemies to give you victory." (Deut. 20:4).*

We need to understand that an eventual Israeli defeat before her enemies would implicitly mean God's defeat before the nations, unless He decides to give the enemies a temporary victory because of the sin of His people. His name, His faithfulness, His grace and His plan for the world would be at stake. This was why Moses' prayer prevailed before the Lord:

*"If you put these people to death all at one time, **the nations who have heard this report about you will say**, 'The LORD was not able to bring these people into the land he promised them on oath; so he slaughtered them in the desert.'" (Num. 14:15-16).*

In other words, Israel has always been God's proxy in the world arena to reveal His glory to the nations. So when Israel is in danger or in pain, our main concern should be for the reputation of the God of Israel in the eyes of the nations:

*"My bones suffer mortal agony as my foes taunt me, saying to me all day long, 'Where is your God?'" (Ps. 42:10).*

David's true motivation of his prayers was not only for the defense of His people but he was grieved at the very thought that a defeat might be interpreted by the nations as a result of God's weakness or abandonment of His people. David's testimony was to make God's glory and character manifest to the nations. Nowadays there is almost a concerted effort among the nations to sever the last bonds connecting them to the Lord and to biblical values. Therefore it is not surprising to see them angry at the only nation officially bonding itself to the God of Abraham, Isaac and Jacob. Israel is probably the sole nation in the whole world that gives a gun and a copy of the Old Testament to every soldier who starts his military service. When the Israeli soldier goes to battle, he knows he does it in keeping with God's purpose and he is therefore assured of the Lord's victory. There are many attempts to pull the Israelis away from the heritage left by their forefathers, but on the other hand there are also growing efforts to preserve this heritage as a protection and a guaranty that God will always be on Israel's side as long as the Jews acknowledge Him as their God. Yet the attacks of the enemies of Israel are often their way to rebel against God and oppose His plans:

*"The kings of the earth set themselves, and the rulers take counsel together, against the LORD and against His Anointed, saying, 'Let us break their bonds in pieces and cast away their cords from us.'" (Ps. 2:2-3, NKJV).*

Although *His Anointed* can be understood as the Messiah it is also meant to be the Jewish people as we see on verse 3: *"Let us break their bonds"*. In other words, when God's enemies seek to *take counsel against the Lord* they become enemies of His people Israel, and this is exactly what is unfolding under our eyes today in the Middle East conflict. However God also uses Israel as a tool in His hands to take revenge on His enemies:

> *"You are my war club, my weapon for battle — with you I shatter nations, with you I destroy kingdoms," (Jer. 51:20).*

The book of Zechariah should be an eye opener for the nations as the prophet foresaw their deliberate attack on Israel before the Messiah's second coming. The sequence of events is as follows:
- The nations will be gathered to fight against Jerusalem (Zechariah 14:2)
- The Lord will fight against the nations (Zechariah 14:3)
- He will uphold Zion's cause (Isaiah 34:8)
- The Lord will put His feet on the Mount of Olives east of Jerusalem. (Zechariah 14:4)

By the way, the Palestinians have clearly stated that, whenever they are given their Palestinian state, no Jew will be allowed in it, let alone in East Jerusalem. What they may ignore is that, when Yeshua comes back on the Mount of Olives, He will still be called *the Lion of the Tribe of Judah*, a Jewish tribe. Even into eternity, Yeshua will not strip Himself of His Jewish identity and the names of the 12 tribes of Israel will still be at the top of each gate in the New Jerusalem. Since the nations are prophesied to attack Jerusalem before the Lord's coming, it is compelling for every believer to pray that his nation may not take any part in this attack. For some of us who have some doubts concerning the Zionist character of the end time prophecies, God's purpose to rebuild Zion is worthy of our close attention:

> *"The nations will fear the name of the LORD, all the kings of the earth will revere your glory. For the LORD will rebuild Zion and appear in his glory." (Ps. 102:15-16).*

Christians ought to know their Bible and remember the end times prophecies. It can be quite challenging to grasp the reasons of the western Church's rejection of Israel in history and partly today. Moreover, it is obvious that these reasons stand as stumbling blocks on the way to a necessary reconciliation between the Jewish people and the Church. On the other hand, it is also interesting to notice how prompt the Church in the third world is to receive the message of Israel in God's plan, how thirsty these Christians are for everything that pertains to Israel and the Jewish people. Because of the adversity and the hardships they endured in their countries, they are more capable to relate naturally to the sufferings of the Jewish people, and to respond with a characteristic love and prayer burden. However the Western Church seems comparatively reluctant to connect with Israel's affliction. Historically, as Jews went through the furnace of affliction, they drew the contempt of the world, as it was actually foretold in the Bible:

> *"I will make them abhorrent and an offense to all the kingdoms of the earth, a reproach and*

*a byword, an object of ridicule and cursing, wherever I banish them." (Jer. 24:9).*

With such a refusal to identify with the Jewish people's sufferings, the Western Church is reluctant to confront the possibility that she too might have to go through the same birth travail in anticipation of her call:

*They preached the good news in that city and won a large number of disciples. Then they returned to Lystra, Iconium and Antioch, strengthening the disciples and encouraging them to remain true to the faith. "We must go through many hardships to enter the kingdom of God," they said. Acts 14:21-22*

She has a tendency to see herself as the Laodicea Church did: she is rich but needs to buy gold from the Lord. She thinks she can see, yet she desperately needs eye salve from her Saviour, but how can she buy it? The way might be painful but it is exemplified by the agonizing history of the Jewish people who has become the mockery of the whole world. If this assumption is right, it seems that this Church puts on her triumphant mask while denying the very path to this triumph which is displayed by Israel's distress. Consequently a great part of the western Church has an inclination to loathe God's discipline and thorny path. It refrains from paying the price for the ineffable role that God has for her. Yet this path invites her to follow the Jews as God's suffering servant:

*O LORD God Almighty, how long will your anger smolder against the prayers of your people? You have fed them with the bread*

191

*of tears; you have made them drink tears by*
*the bowlful. You have made us a source of*
*contention to our neighbors, and our ene-*
*mies mock us. Psalms 80:4-6*

This is what God is causing Israel to endure under the pressures of the nations at the present time. The governments of the world seek to push her into decisions that would make her deny her call and would lead her to compromise, especially on the topic of the land. Would this compromise be what the Church is ready to accept? On the other hand Israel has shown a remarkable capacity to go through the fire of trials, clinging to a land where dangers and threats abound. This said, isn't the Church conscious of its call to lead the world into God's kingdom? It is also a call to reign with Her Lord over the nations in full humility. It is a call to influence our communities in all spheres of life, be the head and not the tail, exactly as Israel was promised to be:

*"The LORD will make you the head, not the*
*tail. If you pay attention to the commands of*
*the LORD your God that I give you this day*
*and carefully follow them, you will always be*
*at the top, never at the bottom." (Deut. 28:13).*

Yet the ways to achieve this goal have been distorted and have become very controversial. Isn't a great part of the Church investing all her skills to please and attract the world to her? Some church services have become show business performances whose goal is only to make them more attractive to worldly people than the church next door. Some preachers have become show managers and God's servants have become actors on a stage. Genuine sincerity of heart has been sold to be politically, socially and immorally correct. By acting this way, this kind of Church is forfeiting her love to her God, her allegiance to His word and her challenge to make Israel envious. She resembles queen Vashti who, because of her pride had rebelled against her king and sought a glory of her own. On the other hand Esther, after much searching of heart, decided to run the ultimate risk on behalf of God's people:

> Then Esther sent this reply to Mordecai: "Go, gather together all the Jews who are in Susa, and fast for me. Do not eat or drink for three days, night or day. I and my maids will fast as you do. When this is done, I will go to the king, even though it is against the law. **And if I perish, I perish**." Esther 4:15-16

Although Esther was of Jewish descent, she symbolizes the hesitation of God's Church concerning her eventual adherence to Israel today, as many Christians are weighing the price to pay before deciding to stand with the Jewish nation. Yet the Bible offers several glimpses of Gentiles who chose Israel's destiny despite the odds of the hour and Rahab is an astounding example. It is particularly interesting to note that her story is related to the conquest of the land and specifically of her own city:

> "Then Joshua son of Nun secretly sent two spies from Shittim. 'Go, look over the land,' he said, 'especially Jericho.' So they went and entered the house of a prostitute named Rahab and stayed there." (Jos. 2:1).

It is in the framework of the Israelites' endeavours to settle on the land of Canaan that Rahab played a prophetic role. She had no connection whatsoever with the Israelites but she heard of them and of what God did on their behalf. She had to take a wise decision for herself and her family and she confronted reality with perfect lucidity:

*"Before the spies lay down for the night, she went up on the roof and said to them, "I* ***know that the LORD has given this land to you*** *and that a great fear of you has fallen on us, so that all who live in this country are melting in fear because of you." (Jos. 2:8-9).*

How could she possibly know this kind of information if not by pure faith?

*"By faith the prostitute Rahab, because she welcomed the spies, was not killed with those who were disobedient." (Heb. 11:31).*

This is a clue for the Church within the context of the Middle East conflict. It is by faith in the relevance of God's word for our days that Christianity can avoid the danger that Rahab so cleverly averted, for it is perilous for the Church to believe the enemy's lie: the division of the land to the Gentiles. It was indeed an inspired, perhaps irrational decision that Rahab took, but one could argue that she actually didn't have any other option and she knew she would die in the slaughter when the Israelites would attack. Yet she could have easily turned the Jewish spies in to the leaders of the city and thwarted their plan, thus keeping the precious intelligence information about the city from reaching the Israelites' commanders, but she chose to believe the spies' promise:

> *"'Our lives for your lives!' the men assured her. 'If you don't tell what we are doing, we will treat you kindly and faithfully **when the LORD gives us the land**.'" (Jos. 2:14).*

For the Church, the promise comes from one with much greater authority than the Jewish spies:

> *But on Mount Zion will be deliverance; it will be holy, and the house of **Jacob will possess its inheritance**. The house of Jacob will be a fire and the house of Joseph a flame; the house of Esau will be stubble, and they will set it on fire and consume it. There will be no survivors from the house of Esau." The LORD has spoken. Obadiah 17-18*

In Rahab's case and to her knowledge, the risks were high. Now she had to decide to uproot herself and her family from her own culture and background to live among a foreign nation. Countless questions must have assailed her thinking about her future destiny. Yet her faith was highly rewarded: she, a former foreign prostitute, became an exemplary mother and entered the genealogy of the Jewish Messiah:

> *"Salmon the father of Boaz, **whose mother was Rahab**, Boaz the father of Obed, whose mother was Ruth, Obed the father of Jesse, and Jesse the father of King David." (Matt. 1:5-6).*

It was the same Boaz who, in such a prophetic way, offered so much hope to another foreign woman named Ruth:

*"'He will renew your life and sustain you in your old age. For your daughter-in-law, who loves you and who is better to you than seven sons, has given him birth.'" (Ruth 4:15).*

Accepting the surrounding situations and refusing the prevailing worldly opinions was a challenge for Ruth as it is for the western Church in our time. Consequently it is not surprising that part of the Church tends to so easily adopt replacement theology and the rejection of Israel in God's plan, but Israel, despite her running away to her many lovers, confronts this Church with her own behaviour today. Would it be right to say that Israel has become the mirror of the Church in which many Christians refuse to look? Would this be why the Church dismisses Israel as a messenger from God to her, or perhaps as a symbol of her sanctification process through adversity, and even the risk of becoming a stench to the world around her? Today both Israel and the Church are confronted with a dilemma and they need to choose: on the one hand faithfulness to their common roots, their forefathers, their call and their husband, on the other hand surrender to the pressures of a humanistic *common sense*. For the time being it looks as though Israel has chosen the most ostracized and strenuous way, but should we cast the stone to the Western Church? Only God can judge her. Wanting to be accepted can be as natural as breathing and it is only by God's grace that we can follow His steps. He has to plant in us a supernatural desire to choose His way in opposition to human reasoning, but for this we need an open heart and a sincere yearning to do His will:

*"I want to know Christ and the power of his resurrection and* **the fellowship of sharing in his sufferings, becoming like him in his death,** *and so, somehow, to attain to the resurrection from the dead." (Phil. 3:10-11).*

God's only way for the Church is to die to herself and to the compromises of this world. It is also to adhere to her companion Israel in order to draw the Jewish people to the fulfillment of their third and fourth stages of life:

*"Again I ask: Did they stumble so as to fall beyond recovery? Not at all! Rather, because of their transgression, salvation has come to the Gentiles* **to make Israel envious.***" (Rom.11:11).*

Only the Holy Spirit can inspire such a noble call and it is given to those who *overcome,* as stated so many times in the first chapters of the Book of Revelation. This is a battlefield where the Church can have an uncontested victory, but in order to win this battle there is a need to rely on God's word and see it as relevant today as it was in days of old. It is after the Jews see the treasure in earthly vessels obvious in the Church, that they will attain the precious salvation foreseen by the prophets of old. Only then will the Church and Israel be in a position to bring the world the ineffable riches that they will share. Making Israel envious does not mean that Israel has to be put on a pedestal, but it certainly acknowledges the Lord's faithfulness and consistency in dealing with His people. On this battlefield, they will both be able to recognize their common commander in chief as well as their common enemy, but the price, both for Jews and Christians who are willing to run this race, might well be of great suffering. Is God's scourge proportionate to His call and even more to the blessings ahead? Would it be a glimpse to the Church whose calling is so great among the nations, or a reminder of the cost attached to the call? In the light of Israel's ultimate vision to attain her fourth level of life toward the nations, shouldn't a mature Church adopt Samuel's attitude toward the Jewish people?

> *For the sake of his great name the LORD will not reject his people, because the LORD was pleased to make you his own.* ***As for me, far be it from me that I should sin against the LORD by failing to pray for you.*** *And I will teach you the way that is good and right. 1 Samuel 12:22-24*

After all, it was Esther who had access to the king, not Vashti, and it belongs to the born again Christians today to clothe themselves with Esther's courageous spirit and approach the King of Kings in intercession on behalf of their sister Israel. However, intercession for Israel should not be only for her survival but also for her righteousness. The Lord is not satisfied for his bride Israel to be alive and protected; He wants her to be made righteous in Yeshua. He wants her to recover the whole land and the Christians' prayer for Israel should be that of the prophet Isaiah:

> *"For Zion's sake I will not keep silent, for Jerusalem's sake I will not remain quiet, till*

*her righteousness shines out like the dawn,*
*her salvation like a blazing torch." (Is. 62:1).*

God wants Israel to be righteous so that the nations would recognize His doing and He would receive the glory:

*"The nations will see your righteousness, and all kings your glory; you will be called by a new name that the mouth of the LORD will bestow. You will be a crown of splendor in the LORD's hand, a royal diadem in the hand of your God." (Is. 62:2-3).*

This is indeed God's way for the Jewish people to step into their capping call. God's desire is to use the Christians in this venture. The parable of the prodigal son reminds us of Israel and the Church. Israel has been rebellious and disobedient. Indeed she has, so to speak, forsaken the Father's farm while the Church has remained faithful to her Messiah for the last 2000 years. Yet the youngest son, after spending all he had, decided to return to his father and to the farm. This is what Israel is experiencing today, although still to a small degree, in the process of the Jews' progressive salvation, for it is only through Yeshua that they can relate to the Father in an intimate way. Yet in this parable, the second son vented his anger not only at his brother's return but also at the Father's indulgence and pardon. He got so used of being the only son of his father and the only heir in the farm, that the thought of sharing his privileges with his returning brother was unbearable. May the Church not succumb to the same selfish sentiment. We need to perceive that the relationship between God and the Jews is a proxy for the Church to understand the ways God relates to her. This is one of the main reasons why He cannot forsake Israel. It would be the wrong message from Him to His Church. He intends to show us believers that albeit our weaknesses, faults and even sins, He would never break the vessel that He is in the process of shaping in His own hands. He would never again bring the flood upon His church as He did in Noah's time, but He would work in the Church from grace to grace and from mercy to victory as He is still doing with His people Israel.

The Jews are not exclusive in their mission to the nations and many Christians, although having to confront the hostility of their fellow believers in Christ, have already received precious revelations and are working jointly with Messianic Jews to fulfill God's plan, as announced long ago by the prophets.

These Christian believers will have to take a decisive step against all odds and perhaps face the likely opposition of a great part of the Church worldwide. Like Ruth they will turn to Israel and boldly declare:

> But Ruth replied, "Don't urge me to leave you or to turn back from you. Where you go I will go, and where you stay I will stay. Your people will be my people and your God my God. Where you die I will die, and there I will be buried. May the LORD deal with me, be it ever so severely, if anything but death separates you and me." Ruth 1:16-17

As the Church realizes that Israel is fighting the same war for the same husband, union will be but a direct consequence. The enemy knows that unity and cooperation between the Church and Israel will herald his end as well as the second coming of Messiah Yeshua.

As mentioned above, and this is a fact of the present age which can never be stressed enough, millions of Christians have already received divine revelation of their common call with the Jewish people in our days. They have wholeheartedly embraced a steadfast love of and burden for Israel and they recognize the importance of the birth of this nation in the Middle East. They have retrieved the biblical roots of the Church and they know the Jewish customs. They know the rabbinical interpretation of the scriptures while being aware of their stumbling blocks but above all, they are faithful intercessors on behalf of God's people and for His land. They keep alert to whatever God is saying concerning His chosen people. They are fully conscious of their responsibility toward Him as those He has entrusted to stand in the gap for the Jews at such a time as this, despite Israel's ignorance of their intercession. Didn't the prophet see these prayer warriors from afar?

*"I appointed watchmen over you and said, 'Listen to the sound of the trumpet!' But you said, 'We will not listen.'" (Jer. 6:17).*

In the last decade, as the situation in the Middle East has grown increasingly tense, the 24 hour prayer watches for Israel and for the region have multiplied. In intercession these Christians are receiving more light concerning their common call with Israel which, at the present stage, has still a mysterious dimension not yet perceived by the church at large. However, Zechariah 8:23 will sooner or later be fulfilled to the utter dismay and probably the criticism of those whose heart has always been ostensibly remote from the Jewish people, to put it mildly.

On the other hand, many Jews become more and more aware of the Christians' love and prayers on their behalf. This is what they still consider as a new strange phenomenon but it starts to have a fruit-bearing impact on their hearts. The new remnant church whose heart has been circumcised with a love for Israel is rising behind the scene and merges with the Jews who have adopted the Passover Lamb as their Jewish Messiah. Didn't the Torah declare it prophetically?

*"An alien living among you who wants to celebrate the LORD's Passover must have all the males in his household* **circumcised;** *then he may take part* **like one born in the land.** *No uncircumcised male may eat of it. The same law applies to the native-born and to the alien living among you."* *Exodus 12:48-49*

Of course, circumcision should be seen here prophetically and does not have in this case a physical implication but rather a symbolical and spiritual one for the Christians in their relation to the Jews. Indeed these Christians are *like one born in the land* in God's eyes, despite the fact that they cannot officially settle in Israel. It is in this perspective that we can and should interpret Isaiah's verses:

*And foreigners who bind themselves to the LORD to serve him, to love the name of the LORD, and to worship him, all who keep the Sabbath without desecrating it and who hold fast to my covenant — these I will bring to my holy mountain and give them joy in my house of prayer. Their burnt offerings and sacrifices will be accepted on my altar; for my house will be called a house of prayer for all nations." The Sovereign LORD declares — he who gathers the exiles of Israel: "I will gather still others to them besides those already gathered." Isaiah 56:6-8*

Verse 6 does not in any way convey a legalistic meaning but rather a spiritual one. The Sabbath is not supposed to be kept in the same way as the rabbis do, but it has to be understood and lived in the way Paul relates to it in Galatians 4 and Hebrews 4. Because of a mistaken legalistic understanding of these verses in Is. 56, some Christians have taken their distance from Old Testament prophecies for fear of falling into Torah observance, as some drastically advocate. Unfortunately the enemy of our soul has his ways to scare and beguile even God's children, but although the devil is still insatiable in his desire to thwart God's plan, and though he may still win some battles dividing Christians and Jews, blurring the truth concerning God's land, he will ultimately lose the overall war. An army of the Lord's true overcomers, both Christians and Jews, is rising and God's sovereign judgment is coming against those who will have taken His word lightly concerning His people and His land:

*In those days and at that time, when I restore the fortunes of Judah and Jerusalem, I will gather all nations and bring them down to the Valley of Jehoshaphat. There I will enter into judgment against them concerning my inheritance,* **my people Israel***, for they scattered my people among the nations and divided up* **my land.** *Joel 3:1-2*

May no believer in Christ be found in this infamous valley!

# Bibliography

- Lambert Lance. *Jacob I have loved.* Lancaster: Sovereign World. (UK), 2007
- Maltz Steve. *The land of many names.* Authentic Life Style, 2003
- Richman Israel & Chaim Ariel. *Carta's Illustrated Encyclopedia on the Holy Temple in Jerusalem.* Jerusalem: The Temple Institute Carta, 2005.
- Cohen Chuck and Karen. *Grounded. The promised land in the New Testament.*, Petersborough (UK):: Present Day Publishing Ltd, with the permission of Sword Magazine.
- Ekman Ulf. *The Jews people of the future.* Ulf Ekman Ministries, 2006. www.ulfekman.org.
- Bennett Ramon. *Philistine.* Jerusalem: Arms of salvation,1995.
- Burnett Ken: *Why pray for Israel.* Lancaster: Sovereign World, 2009
- Katz Samuel. *Battlegound: Fact and Fantasy in Palestine.*; Steimatzky/Shapolsky, 1985
- Harel Israel. *Enter the rest.* Xulon Press, 2012 (Printed in the USA)
- Charles Spurgeon's sermon: *The Church of Christ.* NPSP 1:213-14
- Wertheim Charlotte. *War on God's people.* Chicester (UK): New Wine Press 2002
- Moriah Miri. *Aligning with the spirit of prophecy.* Ishi Publications, 2011(Printed in Israel).

# End notes

1 Lambert Lance. Jacob I have loved: UK, P.F.I. Edition, 2003. Page 29

2 Steve Maltz. The land of many names. Authentic Life Style, 2003. Page 28.

3 Article posted on 20/6/2012 in "Christianity today": http://www.christianitytoday.com/ct/2012/juneweb-only/john-piper-david-brickner-israel.html?start=1

4 Ariel Israel & Richman Chaim. Carta's Illustrated Encyclopedia on the Holy Temple in Jerusalem: The Temple Institute; Carta Jerusalem 2005. Page 7.

5 Cohen Chuck and Karen. Grounded. The promised land in the New Testament., Petersborough: UK: Present Day Publishing Ltd, with the permission of Sword Magazine. Page 1

6 Ekman Ulf. The Jews people of the future. Ulf Ekman Ministries, 2006. www.ulfekman.org. Page 24.

7 Quoted by Bennett Ramon. Philistine. Jerusalem: Arms of salvation,1995. Page 50.

8 Bennett Ramon: Philistine. Arm of salvation. Jerusalem. 1995. Page 130.

9 Bennett Ramon: Philistine. Arm of salvation, Jerusalem. Page 136.

10 Burnett Ken: Why pray for Israel. Lancaster: Sovereign World, 2009. Page 186.

[11] Wilkinson Paul, associate minister at Hazel Grove Full Gospel Church in Stockport, England, speaking at an interfaith Jewish-Christian roundtable in Jerusalem on the 19th of November 2012. Quoted by "The times of Israel": http://www.timesofisrael. com/at-interfaith-meet -in-jerusalem-a-grim-picture-of-jewish-protestant-relations/

[12] Quoted from the Koran (5:51).

[13] Quoted from the Koran; Excerpt K 9:029, Set 38, Count 101.

[14] Al Qibla, March 23, 1918, as cited by Katz Samuel. Battlegound: Fact and Fantasy in Palestine.; Steimatzky/Shapolsky, 1985. Page 12.

[15] Published on 12/2/2012 by: http://www.israelnationalnews.com/News/News.aspx/162753

[16] The Time of Israel, April 8th, 2013: http://www.timesof israel.com/qatari-emir-opens-fund-for-jerusalems-arab-identity/

[17] Israeli newspaper: Haaretz.com. May 4th, 2011. http://www.haaretz.com/news/diplomacy-defense/ netanyahu-hamas-fatah-unity-pact-is-a-victory-for-terrorism-1.359821

[18] San Remo Resolution: http://www.cbn. com/cbnnews/insideisrael/2010/July/ San-Remo-Resolution-Revisited/

[19] Released from censorship by the I.D.F. archives on holocaust Day 7/4/13; Published on the 8th of April 2013: http://www.ynetnews.com/articles/0,7340,L-4365298,00.html.

[20] "The Anti-Terrorist Fence. Ministry of Foreign Affairs". Retrieved August 3, 2011. Published by the courtesy of: http://en.wikipedia.org/wiki/ Israeli_West_Bank_barrier

[21] Maltz Steve. The land of many names. True Potential Publishing Inc. North American Edition, 2010.

[22] Ekman Ulf: The Jews, people of the future. Ulf Ekman Ministries, 2006. www.ulfekman.org.. Page 54.

[23] Charles Spurgeon's sermon Nr. 28: The Church of Christ. Delivered on Sabbath Morning, June 3, 1855. http://www.spurgeon.org/sermons/0028.htm

[24] Charles Spurgeon's sermon Nr. 28: The Church of Christ. Delivered on Sabbath Morning, June 3, 1855. http://www.spurgeon.org/sermons/0028.htm

[25] Article posted on 20/6/2012 on Christianity today: http://www.christianitytoday.com/ct/2012/juneweb-only/john-piper-david-brickner-israel.html?start=1)

[26] Lance Lambert. Jacob I have loved. Bromley: UK. P.F.I. Edition, 2003. Page 40.

[27] Canon 29, Council of Laodicea, 364 AD.

[28] Harel Israel. Enter the rest. Xulon Press (printed in the USA), 2012. Page 76

CPSIA information can be obtained at www.ICGtesting.com
Printed in the USA
BVOW03s1019051114

373810BV00023B/296/P

9 781628 712452